MW01267616

Praise for
Foundations of Instructional Coaching

Hubner's writing is impactful and actionable for new instructional coaches. All new instructional coaches can benefit from the mindsets explained through this book, but the focus on seeing teachers as individuals who possess their own expert craft to reach the needs of students is pervasive in the first part of the book. Too often new coaches want to assume others taught just like they did, and when they see that's not the case, they try to change the person.

Hubner laid out methods for honoring the individual craft of teachers while increasing the growth mindset in the school through a strengths–based focus. In providing questioning stems for coaching, this book provided a roadmap for a new instructional coach, taking theory into action.

Kyle Craighead
Supervisor of Leadership and Coaching
Sumner County Schools, TN

I recommend this book to educators who are committed to becoming instructional leaders and coaches. Educators will find the book to be a thoughtful reboot of ways to think about elevating teaching and learning. Theory, practice, and strategies give actionable ideas to raise the bar called excellence!

Evan Robb
Principal, Author, Keynote Speaker

Ashley Hubner's *Foundations of Instructional Coaching* is one book that all professionals in the field of education should read. There are valuable key points that are important for educators to adhere to: building relationships and most importantly the term, "kids first!" As a successful coach and effective teacher, Ashley Hubner's insight provides advice and a practical guide to successfully support classroom teachers. This book provides a framework to inspire best practices in coaching and teaching. I encourage coaches, teachers, supervisors, and building administrators who want to improve their pedagogy and create a culture that breeds success to read this book.

Nicholas Edwards
Elementary Principal

Foundations of Instructional Coaching, by Ashley Hubner, is a valuable resource for anyone holding a coaching position in the field of education. Although her stories may not answer every question you might have, her book does provide a compass and a road map for helping individuals understand the importance of relationships and the process of assisting educators build their capacity. In the field of education, we are all coaches; therefore we all are of the need to learn how to lead, support and celebrate all of the great things within people. The steps Ashley uses are clear, concise and easy to follow. Her stories will inspire you and at the same time leave you with the "ah ha" moment, as we have all been there. Great work, Ashley!

Dean Packard
Principal

Foundations of Instructional Coaching is a must–have resource for any instructional coach. In this book, you are provided with the foundation of how to be an effective coach to teachers in your building, without being overwhelmed in the process. Ashley provides a simple, yet empowering approach to the reader by providing strategies that are easy to understand and implement in any educational setting. Ashley's ability to integrate her own personal stories, triumphs, and growth, throughout the book, provides the reader with an understanding of why this work is vital to the success of our students in our classrooms and schools. If you're a coach, whether you are new to the role or a veteran, this book is designed just for you!

Lindsay Titus
Assistant Principal, Mindset Coach and Speaker
Define YOUniversity

Ashley Hubner masterfully articulates the value of the instructional coaching process. She addresses the human connection and relationships that lie at the root of coaching success. Ashley clearly illustrates the positive presupposition needed when working with educators. She challenges the reader to dismiss blame and judgment, and to focus on the educators in the schoolhouse. I appreciate that Ashley keeps it real, as she shares specific stressors, as well as hopeful scenarios she experienced as an instructional coach. I am excited to share this book with our instructional coaches and leaders throughout our school district.

Mary Johnston
Chief Academic Officer of Elementary Schools

It is not often that instructional coaches and support teachers have access to mentors who can provide the comfort and strategies that are drastically needed for those who are brave enough to step out of their comfort zone to live on the island of a support role. As a support teacher of 22 years who has worked as a Reading Specialist, Literacy Coach, mentor, and EL teacher, this book is a must read for all of us on day ONE! It is the mentor we never had. Hubner provides real talk, backed up with practical strategies to help guide us through the tumultuous role that exists in the tasks of the support world. She hits a home run when she says, "Education is about community and collaboration, not judgment and competition." Amen!

Andrea Bitner
ELL Teacher, Author, Speaker

Actionable, authentic and anchored in real life experiences, this book is a must have! Whether you are currently a coach or aspire to be one, Ashley's book is one that you need to keep by your side in your everyday work. Her authenticity as she describes best practices for coaches is not only refreshing but inspiring. Ashley shares real stories and how they inform her practice in such a way that it draws you in while making these steps seem manageable. The strategies she shares are tried and true and can be mixed and matched as you need them. As a fellow coach, this book is full of helpful tips to center my work while navigating a complex educational landscape where it can be easy to feel overwhelmed.

Debra Tannenbaum
Elementary School Technology Coach, Author, Speaker, Blogger

A beautifully written take on the adventure of coaching in education stems from Ashley's wellspring of experience. The instructional coach has evolved from a straightforward problem–solver into a position that supports all stakeholders. Her thoughts on building foundational relationships create a partnership that promotes valuable accountability for the reader. Ashley details intentional scaffolding and how to develop a balanced blueprint to lead with authenticity. She provides significant strategies to help others take ownership of their instruction while demonstrating confidence to advocate for student learning. She concludes by giving a challenge to prioritize healthy self–care and shares inspiring takeaways to put into practice!

Jillian DuBois
Educator, Professional Learning Guide, Author, Illustrator

This book resonates on many levels for me and brings back many fond memories of when I entered coaching and leadership roles years ago. I'm confident that it will resonate with you as well. One thing in particular is how Ashely speaks to and shows us, as readers, the convergence of coaching, promoting quality instruction, and honoring educators as the people they are wherever they may be in the different stages of life. Dignity is such an essential element, and Ashley speaks to the heart of the matter and acknowledges the fundamentals of instruction and of relationships that are timeless. Succinctly stated, this is the book that will advance your coaching practice, impact, and coaching relationships. Get this book today!

Vernon Wright
Speaker, Author, Consultant, Leader

Ashley has encapsulated the life a coach in *Foundations of Instruction Coaching*. Ashley's journey through the role of a coach applies to instruction, technology, curriculum, special education, or any type of coaching of teachers. From walking in and building relationships to digging deep in data and curriculum, this book covers it all. With practical advice and shining examples, whether you are a veteran coach or this is your first time in this role, following Ashley's guidance will lead you to success!

Bill Pratt
Educational Leader

Foundations *of* Instructional Coaching

Impact People
Improve Instruction
Increase Success

Ashley Hubner

Foundations of Instructional Coaching: Impact People, Improve Instruction, Increase Success

Road to Awesome, LLC.

This book is dedicated to my husband, for supporting my dreams and ambitions.

And to my parents, for teaching me love, patience, and grit.

"And now these three remain: faith, hope, and love. But the greatest of these is love."
1 Corinthians 13:13

Table of Contents

I mean every word!

Introduction

If you're reading this book, you are probably a coach or about to become a coach. I hope that you find some comfort, encouragement, and motivation as you read through my stories and the lessons I learned as an instructional coach. The purpose of my book is to connect with people, to let you know you're not alone. Coaching is a messy assignment. Each day is different; each relationship is different. There are good days and bad days. There are days when you feel alone and days when you feel empowered. What we always need to remember is that it's about the *kids*. We do what we do every day to better the educational experience for students. If you aren't in this role to impact students, or if you chose to become a coach simply to get out of the classroom, I challenge you to re–think that decision. I promise, it is a lot easier to worry about you and your twenty to twenty–four kids rather than a whole school. The weight of a campus or multiple campuses is far heavier than one classroom. The load is greater; the heart bears more.

Throughout my years as a coach, I often felt that the progress of the school weighed solely on my shoulders. This is a heavy burden to carry. In my head, I knew this wasn't true, yet it didn't make my heart feel it any less. I often felt that the success of students was directly related to my impact, which is somewhat true and somewhat false. As a coach, you will work very closely with teachers and administration, but you can't control them. You can't *make* adults do anything. However, you CAN *impact* them; with that, there can be change. We all want change for the better, change that stems growth and leads to success.

So, as you read this book, reflect on the things you can impact rather than the things you can't control. I learned this strategy in *The 7 Habits of Highly Effective People: Powerful Lessons in Personal Change* by Stephen R. Covey (2020). If you haven't read this book, I highly recommend it. Through reading his book, my outlook on life, work, and relationships changed greatly. I credit my success as an instructional coach to his seven lessons. Without knowing it at the time, Covey's words prepared me for my coaching journey. This is what I hope for in my book as well. I hope that I can offer you some guidance, preparation, and inspiration. I hope you find that my stories parallel yours, and you can use them as support.

I spent eight years in the public school system as an instructional coach. My first year was the most eye–opening experience. I came to realize what principals see and deal with day in and day out, week after week. I learned that leading a school is much like leading a classroom. Every teacher has their own strengths, weaknesses, needs, and personality.

Some teachers will need more support than others, some will need no support at all. You will have teachers in need of intervention, teachers who are self–sufficient, teachers who hide in the crowd and teachers who run the room. What matters most is how you handle these various personalities, how you treat them, love them, and grow them.

I use the word love because I genuinely loved every teacher I ever worked with, no matter how difficult, stubborn, or exhausting. The only way you can make people move is through genuine, honest relationships. I loved my teachers as I had once loved my students. I saw hope, potential, and success in each of them. My job was to find their hidden potential and push it to a point that they may have hated me for it. But it came out of love, for them and their students. Their success as a teacher positively affected their students' success, and, as I said before, it's all about the *kids*.

Many of the teachers I worked with may read this book and think they didn't need to change anything. They may be wondering, *What is she talking about?* They didn't witness their growth firsthand. I did. The change I saw from my first year as their coach to the last year was impressive. Their growth fed my soul. I was able to watch not only their professional growth but their personal growth as well.

Sometimes, personal growth can be more important than professional growth. A teacher's personality, demeanor, and mental stability can positively or negatively affect a classroom. Have you ever heard the saying "happy wife, happy life"? It's the same for a teacher. A happy teacher equals a happy classroom. My goal as a coach was to ensure teachers not only felt better about themselves but felt encouraged as an educator.

As you read this book, I hope the same for you as well. I hope you find comfort in the idea that your profession is about growth, professional and personal. Your impact will change a school, change teachers and change kids. The arrangement of my book is directly related to my path as an instructional coach. It may not be your specific path, and that's OK. Every coach will take a different path as they grow in their profession. Feel free to read chapters in isolation as they meet your needs or read the book in sequence to follow my journey and development as a coach. In the spaces provided, take notes along the way to reflect on later.

Please know that I do not think my stories are the end all be all. I don't feel I was the most successful coach of all time. Just like teachers and students, we have different strengths, weaknesses, failures, and successes. We need a community. Again, this is the purpose of my book, to give you a community. I often felt alone as the only coach on an elementary campus. I walked a fine line between being friends with teachers and coaching them. Oftentimes, I was stuck in the middle of administrative directives and teachers' beliefs. When life gets hard and you have no one to relate to, it's tough; I get it. Let me be there for you.

Find company within my stories and learn from my mistakes. As you read, grow with me and know that YOU can do hard things too.

Enjoy! ♡ Ashley

Building Relationships
Hustle, Pray, Grow

First Steps

Ninety–nine percent of coaching books will tell you that the most important first step of a coach is to build relationships. That's easy to say, but not always easy to do. Some relationships will develop quickly and some may take years. My easiest teacher relationship happened in minutes. My most difficult teacher relationship took five years. Quick relationships happen naturally. Harder relationships take work. They take reflection, patience, and, oftentimes, prayer.

My first journey as an instructional coach was somewhat easier than my most recent. That will not always be the case for new coaches. Some coaches will attain roles on their current campus, moving from a teaching position to an instructional coaching position; others may relocate to a new campus or district to begin their journey as an instructional coach. Either route has the potential to be easy or hard. There are pros and cons to both, and the ease of either will depend on the relationships.

After five years of teaching in self–contained classrooms, I gained my master's in curriculum instruction. I had the opportunity to serve on many curriculum projects within my district and transitioned into my first role as an instructional coach. My official title was Interventionist, but, unintentionally, I began coaching teachers on best practices for Tier I math instruction and intervention. My relationships with teachers were already built and trust existed, and I, effortlessly, transitioned into a coaching role. However, protecting and developing those pre–existing relationships was more difficult than I had thought. This experience was humbling, to say the least. I learned my first lesson of genuine love for other educators.

As teachers, we often judge each other. Don't pretend you don't! We know the good ones. We know the bad ones. We have those we look up to, respect, and want to be. Then, there are those that we wish did things like us. I learned quickly that these thoughts do not embody relationships. Education is about community and collaboration, not judgment and competition. During my first coaching experience, I often found myself thinking *if they would just...* I found myself judging the teachers' techniques, styles, and choices. My eyes had never seen instruction in other classrooms, and, naively, I thought great things were happening in all the classrooms around campus. I soon found out this wasn't the case. When you leave the classroom, you will learn that what happens "inside your four walls isn't exactly what happens inside other teachers' four walls," as my favorite principal said. Because I didn't agree with every teachers' style, and often thought I knew better, I had to put myself in check. I had to push aside my ego in order to cultivate the relationships I already possessed. Through this experience, I learned two lessons. The first of which was: respect that each teacher has their own unique style.

Irritable or Rigorous

Although a teacher's style may not be your cup of tea, most likely, there are kids out there that will benefit from it, even if we don't expect it. For some kids, that teacher may be just what they need for that school year. You probably have someone in mind right now whose teaching techniques you disagree with and wonder who would want them as a teacher. I've been there, believe me, but I caution you on that thought. I've seen students who absolutely love and adore those teachers and make significant progress in their classes.

I remember a math teacher I had when I was in middle school, I'll call her Mrs. Rocco. I felt like she was always on my case. It was annoying, and I thought she was the unhappiest person ever. Looking back, she probably thought I was a know–it–all brat. Despite all of this, I learned the most math that school year and performed at the top of my class. Her teaching style was definitely not what I would emulate as a teacher yet, as a student, it influenced me considerably. It built my work ethic and motivated me to prove people wrong. Other teachers may have thought Mrs. Rocco was too strict or harsh. They may have disagreed with her tactics. For me, it was just what I needed that year. I was becoming a teenager and beginning to think I knew everything. I needed someone to put me in my place and make me work hard for what I wanted.

Compassionate Accountability

During my first coaching experience, I encountered a math teacher just like Mrs. Rocco. She was old–school, as some might say. Some students flourished in her classroom and some struggled significantly. There were parents that loved her and parents that loathed her. As a coach, I was stuck between wanting to "fix" her and making excuses for her. While I understood her intentions, I also saw how it affected some students. I remember telling my principal, "I can coach her on instruction, but I can't change her personality." You really can't change a person's personality, no matter how hard you try. I had to find a balance between her teaching style and the expectations of my administration. I had to acknowledge her personality and teaching approach to decide how I could move forward with a coaching relationship that would produce the results my administration wished to see.

I started with a hard conversation, which becomes frequent in the role of coaching. I didn't have the luxury of reading *Better Conversations: Coaching Ourselves and Each Other to Be More Credible, Caring, and Connected* by Jim Knight (2015) before walking into this role. I had no training on how to navigate relationships with adults, but I knew this conversation needed to happen.

To my benefit, I had invested time in this teacher. We had a cordial relationship that started with hellos and smiles in the hallway. I followed up with supportive praise and compliments. At one time, she expressed to me that she felt seen by me where, conversely, she had felt ridiculed by others. Because I had built this foundation, when the conversation came about, I didn't drain her bucket. I had invested time and energy to fill her bucket beforehand. You may be wondering if the investment was fake, but it was not. I sincerely gave compliments where I saw them fit. Just because you may not agree with a particular teaching style, doesn't mean there aren't opportunities to give praise. Her anchor charts, organization, and content knowledge were impeccable and worth the notice. Where others might have looked past these things because they were focusing on her weaknesses, I focused on her strengths.

I started the conversation by complimenting her strengths and asking some questions to get her thinking. I brought up a few students who were struggling in her classroom and asked her why she thought they may be struggling. I guided the conversation to analyzing their demeanor and response to her. She wanted to focus on what they weren't doing and blame them for not excelling. I showed her some data from the previous year that clearly showed these students had the skills and potential to perform well in her class. Then we dug into her teaching style compared to their personalities. I think the hardest concept for the teacher to grasp was that her personality was hindering the learning process for some of her students. Some students felt nervous around her because of her gruff persona. She thought her sternness was teaching them responsibility. I agree that teaching students responsibility is important but not at the cost of hurting a student emotionally. Some students are more sensitive than others. Each student has their own personality, learning style, and love language. This is where I found my goal for our coaching relationship, *compassionate accountability*.

Once I accepted her teaching style, I was able to set a focus for our coaching relationship that would allow her to keep her teaching style yet build stronger relationships with students. We started by taking the time to fully understand each individual personality, then found differentiated ways to hold each student accountable without breaking the student–to–teacher relationship. I modeled how to respond to students with love yet still hold them accountable for their actions and work.

Love and Logic (2022) is a good resource for this kind of classroom management and discipline. It is a process by which children learn from their mistakes and accept reasonable consequences. To structure this discipline system in the classrooms, adults set firm limits in loving ways. It's common to use assuring, firm statements to address behavior and accept mistakes as learning opportunities. When children cause problems, adults hand these problems back in loving ways. The child is ultimately responsible to fix their behavior or mistake. Adults provide empathy before describing the consequences or let natural consequences occur. The ultimate goal is to give the child control of their behavior rather than fighting for control with you. This is strategic in balancing your expectations and their motivations.

An example might be, a student forgets to turn in their homework. The natural consequence is it's late. There is no need for the teacher to ridicule the student, just to say, "Thank you for letting me know you don't have it today. You know you can still turn it in tomorrow with late points deducted." The teacher will follow up with this consequence just as they said.

Another example, a little more extreme, is a student refusing to do their work. The teacher could respond, "I love you too much to let you fail. How can I help you in finishing your work?" If the student continues to refuse, the teacher can give a choice, "Would you like to complete it now so that you don't miss (activity or reward), or would you like to do it during (activity or reward) time?" If the student refuses to make a choice, the teacher can assign a consequence. In an empathetic manner, the teacher might say, "I'm sad I won't be able to see what you know. I'll have to give you a zero since you did not complete the assignment."

In this scenario, the student's emotions should be considered. If emotions are high, it might be a good time for the teacher to just step away and give them some space. Once the emotions are regulated, the teacher could re–approach and assess the situation. It's important to also understand the time, place and purpose of what is being asked of the student. Some of these components may change the response of the teacher in the moment. Is the work really worth the battle? If so, continue to try love and logic. If not, let it go. Pull them aside later and have another conversation when they can reason with you.

Together, this teacher and I researched these practices and philosophy. We adapted the strategies to fit our needs within her classroom. We determined what her structure would look like. What would be her go–to empathetic phrases? What was in her bank of typical consequences? When would natural consequences come into play? What were her non–negotiables, and what was she willing to let go?

Judgment would not have served me well in this scenario. I would have accomplished nothing. Instead, by coming in with an open–mind on how to use this teacher's specific teaching style, I was able to find a way to help her build a better emotional environment for students without losing herself as a teacher. Students rose to the expectations, not because she was strict, but because she held them accountable with love. She truly knew her students, and they knew her. They had a mutual agreement of expectations and consequences designed with compassion.

Instead of judging other teachers, grow, develop, and find the strengths in their personal style. Education is about collaboration. We can all learn from one another. If we believe we are better than others or they should teach just like us, then we are restricting the progression of unification. We should celebrate each other's differences and personal techniques, yet create a culture where teachers are challenged to consider contrasting perspectives and methods. As educators, we are reflective practitioners. Challenging someone's opinions, actions, and philosophy is necessary for growth. As coaches, we should embrace a culture of reflection within our campus to help teachers evolve their practice over time.

The second lesson I learned while working to cultivate relationships is: assume inexperience by the teacher rather than rejection. There will be cases when you know, without a doubt, something needs to change. If you genuinely believe there needs to be a significant, immediate change with a teacher's instructional practice, refer to this second lesson. Sometimes, the data is telling you a story or you witness teaching practices that do not provide the best learning environment for all students. In these cases, you will need to lead with love and push for change.

Ignorance is Bliss

There are two things I try to always remember when working with ineffective teachers:

1. While teachers may have good intentions, sometimes their intentions are not implemented well.

2. Typically, if a teacher knows better, they will do better.

These two statements pushed me to coach with love, not judgment. Assuming a teacher truly doesn't understand rather than assuming they *can't* or *won't* removes the feeling of frustration and replaces it with empathy. Instead of judging a teacher, you can COACH the teacher.

No matter what I believed or thought I knew about a teacher, I continued to give them the benefit of the doubt. I woke up each day with compassion and grace, starting fresh with each relationship. This mindset opened many opportunities for me to do my work during my years as a coach. It also helped me to remove unnecessary stress and continue to move forward each day with a positive outlook.

I first learned this lesson while dealing with a teacher who taught the grade level above me following my last year in the classroom. She had a few of my previous students and kept asking for support. I noticed that those students were seriously struggling in her class. They struggled in my classroom the previous year as well. However, by the end of the year, they were successful. As their teacher, I learned that systematic intervention was the key to their success. At first, I thought this teacher just wanted me to do the intervention for her since this was part of my new role. I presumed she lacked the skills needed to intervene. I was frustrated that she couldn't help these students succeed. I kept thinking *if she would just do the intervention, meet with them in small groups, use scaffolding, pre–teach vocabulary, etc.*

I knew, as a coach, I couldn't approach this teacher while I was frustrated. I had to humble myself and assume she didn't know any better. This situation gave me an open opportunity to coach the teacher on the techniques and strategies I had previously used with these students that produced results. Although there was some resistance, eventually, change happened. I don't know 100 percent if I helped the teacher grow her instructional knowledge or if she just conceded to get me out of her hair. What I do know is that she transitioned from not providing intervention at all to providing quality, daily intervention for these students. In the end, the students were learning and growing, despite whatever circumstances got us to that point. This is what coaching is really about: *moving teachers* who *move students.*

Lessons Learned

The old saying, love your neighbor as yourself, is sometimes hard for us to swallow. Yet it is valid and should be practiced, especially, in a role of leadership. The only way to reach people is through genuine care and compassion. I had to learn to love all the teachers on the staff, whether I agreed with their teaching style or not. I had to love the teachers who I thought were neglecting to teach to the best of their ability. I learned to approach teachers with a sincere sense of care and support, rather than judgment.

Sometimes, this compassion is hard to show and words aren't enough. I paid specific attention to my tone of voice, demeanor, and even my wording during conversations. It's easy to send unintentional messages if you are not careful. You don't want people to wonder if you have ill intentions or negative notions. I learned that questioning is always better than telling. If you can get to the root of the problem, you can find a solution together. I was able to collaborate with almost every teacher on my campus because I embodied an open–door policy without judgment. I put my negative thoughts in a box and ignored them. I definitely had opinions and assumptions, but I did not act on them. What we think is not always the reality. To really understand any teacher and to have empathy for their situation is to listen, reflect, and communicate. I firmly believe that to SUCCEED in your role, you must first impact people. This will lead to improved instruction, and improved instruction will lead to success for teachers *and* students. Everyone within a school community should have ACCESS to SUCCESS.

Impact People ⟹ Improve Instruction ⟹ Increase Success

Make An Impression

Fast forward one year later when I found myself as the newbie on a very high–performing campus. Not only was I the newbie, I was the only new hire that school year and the youngest educator on campus. I had a lot of relationships to build and a lot to prove to the staff. As I said earlier, some relationships are easy and some are hard. Some of the teachers took to me immediately which was a relief, and some questioned my experience. As much as we don't mean to judge a book by its cover, it happens. I have dealt with this my whole life. I have what people call a babyface and often get judged because I look young. I knew some of the veteran teachers were questioning my age, skills, experience, and knowledge.

You may find yourself in a similar situation and this is why building relationships is important. You need teachers to trust your judgment, knowledge, and skill–set. You need buy–in to coach, and you need to coach to make an impact. I promise, it may take time, but it is possible!

Traditionally, high–performing schools are hard to coach. What they're doing seems to be working. Why change anything? However, the curriculum was changing, new initiatives were coming, and many teachers were changing grade levels or subject areas. There were a lot of opportunities here; I just needed them to trust me.

My first strategy to build buy–in was to lead a professional development (PD) session on the first day of our teacher work week. It was, literally, my first day on the job. I'm not the most out–going person. I struggle talking to people I don't know. I need to find connections to open up and build relationships. I was hoping that my PD session would help the staff find some connections with me. I led a session about critical thinking and metacognitive skills that I had previously led at a Texas Association of Supervisors of Mathematics (TASM) conference. I believe this first impression set my relationship with the staff off on the right foot. They were able to get a glimpse of my skill set and started to build some trust in me.

To begin the day, I greeted every teacher as they came into my session just like we greet students in the morning at school. I stood toward the entrance of the library and introduced myself to each staff member and shook their hand. This may have impressed some, others may have thought I was an oddball. I'm not absolutely sure, but it was a step toward making connections with people. Although I'm somewhat socially awkward, I do enjoy addressing an elephant in the room, and that elephant was ME. Why not throw myself to the wolves on the first day? Following this first interaction, I had several teachers invite me to lunch, reach out to me for instructional support, and confide in me about their struggles. I was starting to build some solid relationships. To continue the momentum, I used my first week after the students returned to visit teachers' classrooms. I popped in, introduced myself to the students, and left a nice note for each teacher. I saw every classroom within the first week of school. Some teachers were very open to me dropping by, others, not so much. That was OK. I knew, for some, it would take time.

Take a moment to think about the first impression you could make. How could you start the school year off on the right foot? Reflect on your strengths as a leader. Write down some ways you could use these strengths to make a good impression.

Build Confidence

Teaching is a very personal occupation. Teachers take pride in their classroom and instruction. Some are fearful of criticism or objection to their work. Some are insecure and haven't built their confidence yet. Some just don't like the interruption. All of these reasons can make a teacher hesitant to let you in their room.

I remember the first time my principal came to watch me teach. I, literally, froze. Baffled, he stared at me and said, "You can continue." Except, I was in shock. I was nervous that I wouldn't be good enough. I worried that a student would act out, and I wouldn't handle it correctly. Would I teach the lesson right? Would I say the wrong thing?

We're all afraid of being judged and criticized. We all want to do well. It took time for me to realize I didn't have to be perfect. I just had to do my best for the kids. I soon mastered the art of ignorance. Once I learned to ignore my principal when he came into my room, it didn't bother me. Before I knew it, my principal started sending all kinds of people to my room to watch me teach. I pretended they weren't there, and my insecurities left. I just kept doing my thing. I trained my students to ignore them too, except for those circumstances where they asked the students questions. My goal was for us to work as we always worked every day: mistakes, messes, and all. This is a lesson I would share with any teacher. Don't worry about the people coming in and out of your classroom; just do you. What we will see is the reality of teaching, the day–to–day messiness of growing and loving students. Within these moments, I challenge teachers to be reflective and open to feedback in order to perfect their practice.

This is another reason for building relationships. Once you have a relationship with a teacher, they are more likely to be reflective and open to feedback. They are also more likely to invite you into their room. They need to know you aren't evaluative. You aren't judging them. You are only trying to support them and help them grow so students grow.

This brings me back to our earlier discussion about teaching styles. When you really know your teachers, you better understand their style. That only happens by watching them and talking to them. Observation and dialogue are the most helpful tools in really getting to know your teachers. Dialogue helps you understand their intentions. Observation helps you understand their implementation. Sometimes what a teacher wants to accomplish in the classroom may not actually be happening due to underlying circumstances. This offers you a great opportunity as a coach to help the teacher see that their intentions are not the reality.

I think of it like this: when you have a conversation with a person, then you hear them relay that conversation to someone else, is it exactly how you imagined it went? Usually not. Each person has their own interpretation, their own reality of what was said or intended. Although teachers know what they want to happen in the classroom, sometimes outside influences hinder their implementation: clarity of language, student behavior, activity resources, and classroom management, just to name a few. The reason doesn't matter. What matters is finding a solution. Knowing a teacher's style will help you decide how to support them. *What is the one tweak or adjustment we could make to resolve the issue? How could we enhance the teaching implementation to match the intention of the lesson?*

As a coach, you have to build confidence within your teachers and empower them to reflect on their own personal practice. Then, they can internally monitor and adjust their instruction through metacognitive reflection. This practice is built through using every moment with a teacher in the most intentional way.

"Everyone we work with knows a lot more and can do a lot more than we think. It's our job as coaches to find out what it is that they know, care about, can do, and are committed to, and then to use that information to help them move their practice."

~Elena Aguilar

What might be your next steps to get to know your teachers and their craft?

....

....

....

....

....

....

....

....

....

....

....

....

....

....

Reluctant Teachers

We've discussed the initial steps in building relationships and laying the foundation for a coaching partnership. Now, it's time to discuss some of the more difficult components of relationship building. Remember that relationship that took me almost five years to build? It was taxing to say the least, emotionally and mentally draining. However, things that take time aren't always bad. You learn from them, and I learned a lot about myself and about that teacher. The reward in the end was worth all the work.

I think most coaches would agree that working with reluctant teachers is hard. It was a long road to figuring out how to understand some of my teachers. Emotions were heavy–stress, anger, frustration, resentment, anxiety... I had many sleepless nights, spent hours praying, and some nights crying. Every Sunday, when I was at church, I felt like God was telling me to forgive, move on, and start fresh again on Monday. I don't believe these teachers ever knew I felt like this, and if they knew now, I think they would truly feel apologetic.

My feelings stemmed from the disagreeable interactions I had with these teachers. It really had nothing to do with instruction. Sometimes, people are just impolite, and you need to learn how to deal with it. I received huffs, puffs, eye rolls, arguments, demands, and refusals. All of which hurt. No one likes to deal with a disgruntled teacher. Unfortunately, that's our job sometimes.

Coaching Change

What I realized over those years working with those reluctant few is that I was taking their rejection personally and, in the end, I don't think it was me they didn't like. As a coach, we often become the messenger. I was the messenger, the symbol of change: new mandates, new curriculum. These teachers didn't want to change. They didn't want to try a new curriculum or add one more thing to their plate. They wanted to be left alone to do what they had always done. Over time, I began to realize these reluctant teachers could be placed into three different groups associated with their feelings toward change: skeptical, resistant, and insecure.

- *Skeptical* teachers often don't trust the idea of change. They have their doubts about the purpose or need to change.

- *Resistant* teachers usually don't want to do the work to change. They could be tired, overwhelmed, or overworked. Sometimes resistant teachers are content with their current situation, therefore, they don't want to change. They fear the change will bring discomfort.

- *Insecure* teachers doubt themselves, their expertise, and their practice. They are unsure how they will perform with the change.

As you read through the chapter about professional development, you will learn strategies I used to support all of these types of teachers through change.

What all of these teachers need to know and understand is that education is always changing. There is no constant. Education is as progressive as the world around us. There are always new ideas, new resources, and new methods to meet the needs of children. Our children are constantly changing. With each generation, there are new concerns and issues. Our job is to stay current with the most recent research related to curriculum and instruction. This is exhausting and overwhelming for some teachers, even the reason some have left education, yet this is the reality of teaching. Always changing. Always growing. You'll find your most resilient teachers are flexible, adaptable, and embody a growth mindset. If you can foster this culture in your school, I would say you have a win.

"There is always frustration from people who work in schools that things keep changing, but it is an unfortunate truth with the world of work changing as rapidly as it is, we do have to change."

~Jim Knight

Response Strategies

I think the hardest thing about being a coach and building relationships is being quick on your feet to respond, especially when dealing with reluctant teachers. Let me tell you, it took a lot of practice and reflection to craft my response strategies. While we hope that every educator is pleasant every day; that is not the case. Teachers have bad days too and, as the coach, you're usually the one to hear about it. I have been yelled at, cried at, and completely ignored. This can be emotionally and mentally draining for a coach. Learning how to deal with these situations and react appropriately was quite the journey for me. I laughed; I cried; I even froze in shock! I had to learn how to compose myself and choose my words carefully in several circumstances.

Some of our best teachers can be the hardest to deal with. They are passionate about their work, and they don't hold back. Some teachers fear change, and when you turn their world upside down, you better be ready for the aftermath. The worst is forced change. We, the coaches, cannot control these circumstances. The only thing we can control is how we respond to these situations. Some of the best leaders in my past taught me some strategies to deal with these various situations:

- *One–liners*
- *Data Digging*
- *Questioning*

One of the best tips came from a friend in administration. Her tip was to have one–liners prepared that offer support but don't undermine the administrative decision at hand. Her go–to response was, *"What can I do to help you accomplish this? How can I support you?"* This shows teachers that you can't change the situation, yet you are willing to support them in any way necessary. You have no control of what is being asked of them, you only have control of how to support them. You are not validating them, nor dismissing them. You are staying focused on your job: coaching.

Usually, in these circumstances, teachers don't know or see the reasons why. Most of the time, it is something bigger than them and their classroom. It could be due to a campus or district need based on data, observations, or community feedback. This is hard for teachers to grasp because they only see what happens in their classroom. If they are good, confident teachers, it is even harder for them to understand. This may be a hard situation for you and leads me to my second tip: *Data Digging*.

A smart administrator once told me, let the data speak for itself. You can't argue with the numbers. Data can show the bigger need. It's kind of like life. We don't know that there is a huge need somewhere else out in the world if we don't ever turn on the TV or browse the internet. If we are only worried about what happens in our household, then nothing in the world would ever change. We wouldn't even know there was a problem. Articles, commercials, talk shows, and the news all present data that shows various needs around the world. Once we know there is a problem, we want to help. When we see a need, we want to fix it, no matter how small the contribution might be.

I recommend using data to show teachers the bigger need. Challenge them to see their opportunity to support the bigger picture. Push teachers to self–reflect and evaluate their own strengths and weaknesses based on the numbers in front of them. Data can be black and white, clear and specific. I say *can be* because there's always a deeper story to each child's data that cannot be seen in just numbers. I believe children should be evaluated holistically, considering the whole–child, not just through test scores. However, in efforts to evaluate a BIG picture, data is very helpful. Teachers can globally evaluate strengths and weaknesses by comparing across their grade level, district, or state. Finding trends will help them see the whole picture.

Still, teachers may struggle with seeing exactly what you want them to see. They may get off on tangents. When this happens, I refer to another good tip: *questioning*. Questioning, in this case, needs to be pre–planned. Just like we ask teachers to pre–plan questions for lessons of inquiry, we should pre–plan our questions to guide teachers in discovery. Prepare to ask questions about the data that guides teachers to see the bigger picture.

- Did you notice...?
- What do you think about…?
- What do you think... means?

These are great questions for guiding teachers to self–reflect and analyze data. It's specific and observational. When teachers see the specific need, then you can move to the planning process. Try using some of these question stems to encourage teachers to make a plan for the change that needs to happen:

- What do students need?
- How could we…?
- When will we…?

5 Whys Analysis

The best in – the – moment response I could offer a new coach is *questioning*. **Why**, is one of the best. The Toyota company used the idea of 5 Whys

(2022) to find the root cause to issues they faced when implementing new products. The 5 Whys Analysis is a technique you can use to get to the foundation of a problem. Sometimes the source of the p r o b l e m i s unexpected. This is why it's important to stop and reflect through the 5 Why process to find the root cause of the problem and solution within their control. Other question stems that can support the 5 Why process could be: *Can you tell me more? Can you explain further?*

Continue to ask why until the answer becomes clear.

A clear answer is:
- *Controllable*
- *Action–oriented*
- *Manageable*
- *Attainable*

Sometimes when a teacher is upset and frustrated, this is the easiest way to calm them down. It gives them time to stop and think. They can process their feelings, explain themselves, and begin to feel some emotional release. With these question stems, just like the one–liners, you aren't validating their feelings or dismissing them. You are just questioning and listening. They are doing the talking and thinking. Most of the time, this strategy helps me get to the root of the problem. Once I have found the root, I can then offer some collaborative solutions that will support the teacher and give them some peace of mind.

I once had a coach that used questioning as her go–to method. At first, I found it quite annoying. In my mind, I came to her for answers, suggestions, and solutions. She was trying to lead me to the water, not give me the water. Even though she never told me her opinion, I knew what it was by the way that she asked the questions. Her specific and intentional questioning guided me to creating solutions aligned with our campus goals.

After a while, I began to think through these questions on my own, without even going to her. She was teaching me to be an independent, critical thinker and self–reflector. I didn't need her as much to show me the ways. I began to figure them out for myself. This is the ultimate goal of any coach, for teachers to become independent in self–reflection. We want them to become self–motivated to find solutions, analyze data, and make changes to their practice. So, although it was annoying at first, it molded me into the educator and coach that I am today.

Questioning is a fundamental skill for a coach to learn. If you haven't mastered this yet, start by writing three to four question stems to use and post them somewhere you can see them. Refer to them when having a conversation with a teacher. The more you practice, the more of a habit it becomes. Through the Resources QR code, you will find response tools and a data analysis toolkit.

What response strategies will you add to your coaching toolkit? What one–liners can you develop and practice? What questions will you implement in your practice?

Small Moments Count

When all else fails, remember to use every moment with a teacher in a very intentional way. One of the biggest outbursts that I dealt with was a teacher who was asked to change subject areas days before school started. She was irate, as you could imagine. All her summer professional development had been in another content area. Her room was already set up; she had lesson plans ready. Her world was turned upside–down. She came into my room screaming, crying, cursing. So much so, I could barely even understand what she was ranting about. I just kept repeating, "Slow down. Take a breath."

After a few minutes, she finally calmed down enough that I could understand what she was saying. I asked her to explain what was going on; explain to me *why* she was upset. I just let her talk. After a while, I asked her *why* she thought this decision was made. She said, "Because she [the principal] knows I can do it." The principal had confidence in her to be the best fit for the job. Data supported the principal's decision. She was making a choice for the good of the students. Did this decision come at the ideal moment? No. Was the teacher thrilled about this change? Absolutely not. However, my job was to support this decision. I reassured her that I was there and would help her.

By the end of the conversation, the teacher was fine. She knew it would all be OK; she just needed to process the situation and deal with her emotions. Special moments like this, although hard, will never be forgotten by a teacher. They will remember how you listened, how you helped them see, how you supported them. These moments build trust, and authentically develop a true partnership.

Our job is *not* to make the decisions but to make sure they are implemented in ways that grow teachers and students. Our job is to make sure everyone is on the team. We need everyone to be all in, every day, for kids. It's all about the kids. The more that we have moments like this with the teachers, the more they will buy–in to the focus on student success. It's not about you. It's not about them. It's about the kids. If we can get every teacher to believe in us, then we can create an environment where, as Todd Whitaker (2013) says, it's "cool to care." Behaviors and beliefs are tied to emotions. If teachers are as emotionally invested in you, as you are in them, then they are willing to change and adjust, willing to go above and beyond. So, use every moment to its fullest. Influence each and every teacher in whatever ways possible, build those

relationships, and impact change. As you read through the rest of this book, you will notice that the basis of all my decisions, intentions, and actions is RELATIONSHIPS. Each coaching move I make is in an effort to Impact People which Improves Instruction and Increases Success!

"The Coach is not a problem solver, a teacher, an advisor, an instructor, or even an expert; he or she is a sounding board, facilitator… who raises awareness and responsibility."

~John Whitmore

Reflections & Takeaways

Professional Development
Are You Listening?

Supporting Teachers Through Change

Working with reluctant teachers is hard. As much as we want to support them, sometimes it's difficult to figure out a way that works. We want to protect the relationship, but also implement the change handed to us. I approached my reluctant teachers with a growth mindset, for them and myself. Together we could grow through the change. I was vulnerable and honest about the process and used strategies that supported them along the way. Think of it like teaching. Those hard to reach students often want someone to love and support them. We scaffold their learning to make it easier. We give them time, attention, and support. With my teachers it was the same. It took time, effort, and lots of love, and, eventually, I won them over. They began to differentiate their relationship with me as their coach from the changes coming from administration. Their reactions were more subdued. They didn't want to kill the messenger anymore. I received more buy–in and more willingness to try new things because I found ways that worked for them.

How did I build this growth mindset culture with these teachers? Here are a few techniques you could use when releasing new information to teachers that will help scaffold their learning and understanding along the way.

Simplify it

Strategically weed out the unnecessary information and limit dispersal of new information on a need–to–know basis. Teachers only need to know what pertains directly to them and their grade level. Teachers, also, don't want to sit through unnecessary meetings. With this in mind, make each interaction purposeful by using your time efficiently. Try differentiating your meetings, trainings, and Professional Learning Community (PLC) gatherings to meet the specific needs of varying teacher groups. Show them how the new information will specifically affect their classroom and practice by outlining the most important components related to the new information.

Bridge it

Bridge the old to the new. Take the current practice and relate it to the new practice, highlighting the major and minor changes. This gives teachers a visual of how they could adjust their current practice without starting over completely. Work together to find solutions in adjusting to the new without losing teacher identity. Teachers still want control, ownership, and craft within their teaching. If we take these away completely, we will lose our teachers. Work with your teachers to find ways to integrate their current teaching styles with these new expectations.

There is always wiggle room with any new initiative. The key is to find where the choices are hidden. With a reading curriculum, it might be the book choice. If a teacher is passionate about *James and the Giant Peach*, then let them use *James and the Giant Peach* to teach the new reading curriculum. If a teacher is passionate about free choice seating, then let them find a way to allow this option without changing the classroom management expectations. Find what the teacher believes they cannot live without and blend it with the new system.

Chunk it

Separate the new information into a gradual release timeline to chunk the amount of information teachers will be receiving throughout the semester, term, or year. Prioritize the information and decide how and when you can release this information to teachers. Some examples might be: breaking it up over three weeks in PLC meetings or releasing some information in an email, follow-up in a staff meeting, and concluding in a PLC. You must decide what method of communication and delivery will work best with your staff.

Each timeline I created to disperse new information was purposeful and intentional. By chunking the new information, teachers did not feel overwhelmed. They had time to process chunks of information before adding more to it. I thought of it as a ladder or staircase. What first step do my teachers need to conquer before moving on to the next one? We mastered the first step, then moved to the next and continued our way up the ladder until we had mastered it all.

These methods helped me lighten the load for my teachers. I hope it prevented some stress and helped teachers see that they could do it. In conjunction with these methods, I tried to remember to build confidence within my teachers, encourage them, and motivate them. I continually complimented their efforts. The goal through these new initiatives was not perfection but practicing to perfect our instructional practice within the classroom. If they tried and failed, I was proud anyway. I was proud that they gave the effort and took a risk. I was there to help them get back up and try again. I continued to highlight their strengths and coach their weaknesses. I gave them praise for continuing to implement their strengths within the classroom as they muddled through the new. I wanted them to know that I still saw an amazing teacher no matter how defeated or unsure they may have been feeling through this process.

With time, people change. Going through a journey together builds relationships. There may be tears, anger, and frustration along the way. But when you make it to the end, it feels great. I think now my reluctant teachers would say they appreciated me. Through the process of change, we learned to lean on each other, which grew us closer together. They may have hated me at times, but they are professionally and personally better for it, and so am I. My best advice would be to keep your eyes on the big picture. Keep moving forward, and, eventually, they will come too.

What strategies do you think will be helpful in supporting your teachers? How could you use these strategies in upcoming learning opportunities?

Presentation Techniques

There are many different avenues through which we will coach teachers. It may be one–on–one in a coaching partnership. It may be through meetings and trainings. As an instructional coach, professional development is usually included in your job assignment. I spent several years serving on the math curriculum team and providing math professional development. I experienced professional development opportunities that ranged from small groups of 10–15 to large groups of 50–100. Although I enjoyed small groups better, I found myself leading professional development opportunities with larger audiences. This came with heaps of fear and room for growth.

Public speaking has always been a fear of mine. I'm sure other teachers can agree. It's easy to talk to kids, but talking to adults is a different story, especially when you're standing in front of 50–100 teachers at one time and all eyes are on you. I was worried about what people would think. What would they say? Would I do a good job?

I began learning from my administrators, listening and watching the way they spoke, how they handled themselves, how they responded to audience members. I quickly learned you don't have to be perfect, and you don't have to know all the answers. You just have to be you, authentically and honestly. Adequate preparation, practice, and intentional design can support you in implementing a smooth professional development session. Over time, I learned processes that helped me become efficient in creating and implementing professional development. My stage–fright disappeared because I felt prepared and equipped to teach teachers.

I can summarize my process into two categories: *planning* and *preparing*. I created my own list of reminders to refer to when planning and building a professional learning opportunity. This part is important to ensure your audience will get the most out of their learning opportunity.

Planning Considerations:

- **Be Intentional:** Use explicit instruction and language. Make sure your message is clear and direct.

- **Engage Your Audience:** Find ways to keep your audience on task and engaged in the learning experience.

- **Make it Real:** Model the learning and present it in a realistic, applicable way.

- **Equity:** Provide equal, accessible opportunities for all participants to engage with the content.

- **Pre–Planned Questions:** Think about the questions your audience might ask and pre–plan your answers to those questions.

Preparing for a professional learning opportunity is just as important as planning for one. Using the two tips below you can assess your time management and the clarity of your message. This will also allow you to reflect and adjust before implementing a new PD.

Preparation Tips:

- **Script your PD:** Use your own personal language style to write out, explicitly, what you will say during each portion of the presentation. This is a good way to process your thinking and bring clarity to your message.

- **Act out your PD:** Present to a friend or co-worker to receive feedback and make adjustments before presenting. You might consider giving them a checklist of specific components you want to assess. See my sample checklist in the Resources.

What are your actionable next steps to planning professional learning?

Engagement Strategies

Do you ever wonder if people are even listening to you when you present? I have wondered this many times. Once, I positioned myself directly behind a teacher who I believed was not paying attention. When I looked at her computer screen, she was shopping on Amazon! I could not believe my eyes. A grown adult, blatantly not paying attention. I've had other experiences with people sleeping during the PD or just ignoring me all together, not even acknowledging my existence.

The thing is, you can't control adults. All you can do is control yourself and how you react to these situations. I learned many tips and tricks from the book, *Lemons to*

Lemonade: Resolving Problems in Meetings, Workshops, and PLCs by Robert J. Garmston and Diane P. Zimmerman (2013). I highly recommend this book for any new coach. It is filled with a multitude of reaction strategies and recommendations for handling difficult situations that may occur during any professional learning opportunity. The book explains that we really don't know what is going on in people's lives or what they are thinking about. Although it may seem like they are being rude, it may not have anything to do with us at all. One of the best lessons I learned was to ignore the audience.

Have you heard the term RBF? If not, I'll put it nicely. It refers to someone who seems to always have a frown on their face and their eyes squinted, as if they are constantly irritated or dissatisfied. You have probably experienced some of these people before. I encountered several during some of my first experiences leading professional development. At first, I took it personally. I thought, *"This teacher hates me."* However, *Lemons to Lemonade* suggests that the teacher could be thinking really hard, concentrating on what you're saying, or processing the new information. The teacher could be thinking about a situation at home or outside of work. Maybe something is going on in their personal life that they are struggling with and they are worried. Or maybe they just have RBF. We will never really know and rather than take it personally, just ignore them and continue on with your presentation.

Although it is important to you, sometimes your PD is not the most pressing matter in someone else's life. You can't control this. Maybe that Amazon–shopping teacher I mentioned earlier had just been told she's changing grade levels, and she was frantically looking for materials and resources for her new job assignment. Maybe she just wasn't engaged in my session. You never really know what is going on with anyone, so don't take it personally.

If you don't feel you can ignore the situation, then I would suggest approaching the participant, privately, with genuine curiosity and questioning them about their disengagement. Confront them in a consoling manner that intends to assist them, not to judge them. Kindly ask them if there is something you can do to support them or ask if they have a concern they would like to express. Usually, teachers will be honest and explain what is going on. Sometimes, they may make up an excuse. Either way, you now have their attention and maybe some validation that their issue is not with you or your presentation.

Ultimately, the responsibility of learning is on the participant. When people truly want to engage and learn, they will. While we can't force people to participate or engage during any presentation, we can influence participation. Just like teachers encourage engagement in the classroom, we can encourage engagement during professional learning. Here are some strategies for encouraging engagement and holding participants accountable as you present your professional learning session.

- **Present an Agenda:** Allow participants to view the scope of the day at the beginning of the session; this gives them time to process what the day will look like.

- **Chunk Your Presentation:** Structure your presentation into three to four main goals/learning experiences. This gives the audience time to process learning, take breaks, and organize notes.

- **Incorporate Collaboration:** Use strategies such as table talk, think–pair–share, or hands–on activities to keep the audience engaged and focused on the learning

- **Allow Processing Time:** Give the audience time to take a break and process their thinking. This may include conversations with teammates, reflecting on notes, and/or summarizing their learning for the chunks of the presentation.

- **Create a Task:** Give attendees a task to complete at the end of the session or following each specific portion. This holds the audience accountable for their learning. It gives incentive for them to listen and pay attention. To make it more purposeful, try to incorporate a task that directly ties back to their classroom, something they can take and use immediately following the presentation.

Feedback & Reflection

Another important concept of professional learning is self–reflection. In your role, it is important to take feedback and learn from your experience. We should always have a growth mindset as a coach. There is constantly room to grow.

Offer audience members the opportunity to reflect on their learning experience and give feedback on the presentation. Just like students, teachers want to be heard as well. Give them the opportunity to share their thoughts. Have an open mind as you read participants' responses, suggestions and criticism. Take it all with a grain of salt. Find the truth behind the comments. You will find praise and concerns. Some comments will be allusive; some will be direct. Within all of the feedback, identify your areas of strength and areas for growth. Set goals for yourself and reminders for your next presentation.

Consider how you would like to dissect the data collected within your questionnaire. You might like using ratings, multiple choice options, or open–ended questions. A mixture of two or more may allow you to see trends within the data. Cover an array of presentation areas to grasp data for an overall experience. Topics might include:

- Overall Experience
- Quality of Presentation
- Engagement in Activities
- Interest Level of Content
- Organization of Information
- Communication & Delivery
- Other Comments, Suggestions, Concerns, or Questions

This last suggestion is important. Make sure you give participants the option to add their feelings about the presentation. When participants leave a question for you on your survey, be sure to follow up with them and respond to their questions. This shows attendees that you sincerely care about their concerns which helps with building relationships.

Reflections & Takeaways

PLCs
It's Not About You

Professional learning community meetings are another form of professional development. Coaches should be able to support teachers through this process. Depending on the teachers' levels of knowledge related to PLCs and the relationships among the team, your role may look different from grade level to grade level, team to team. I've been the leader, the facilitator, and the observer depending on the PLC. Some teams were efficient and others needed much more guidance. An efficient, strong PLC is the most effective professional learning tool that directly affects student growth. This is where the hard conversations happen. Data–driven, reflective practitioners learn, grow, and thrive in the PLC and return to the classroom to impact students in the most positive way.

If you don't know what PLCs are, I strongly recommend looking into Solution Tree (2022) as a resource. They offer great training and resources for PLCs. For teachers to grow and impact student learning, you need quality, functioning professional learning communities. This should be a safe place for teachers to reflect, dialogue, and plan for student success.

Not all teachers are receptive to the idea of PLCs. In fact, most of my teachers initially despised PLCs. They saw it as one more meeting; therefore, it was not useful to them. We tried to create campus buy–in by designing a focus for our PLCs. We created structures, provided choice, and offered a generous amount of support. Through these actions, we coached teams to become more efficient in PLCs. Soon, most teachers saw purpose in our PLCs and realized that it was a time to collaborate, share their voice and problem–solve solutions. There were still naysayers, and, like I said before, you can't control adults or force them into anything. In the end, the decision is theirs to be an active, engaged participant, and if they choose not to use the PLC in a purposeful way, it's their loss.

Focus Lens

PLCs are NOT a time to gripe, complain or vent. They are not a time to check emails, make phone calls, or work on lesson plans. Sometimes, we get lost in the day–to–day worries and struggles and lose track of our priorities. It's easy for teachers to stray from the intended focus of PLCs and get bogged down with all the daily events. As coaches, we need to refocus those conversations on student success and growth. Students should be the focus of all our decisions, especially, for any and all professional learning opportunities such as PLCs.

Complaining, tangents, personal struggles, and scheduling conflicts can all become barriers to a productive PLC. There needs to be a team member who can redirect the focus back to students. This may be a strong teacher on the team, you (a coach), or an administrator. It doesn't matter who supports teachers in staying focused on student learning; it just needs to happen. Here are some examples of how you can support teams in student-centered PLCs.

Teacher's Comment	Coach's Response
I don't know why we are talking about this, my students can't do that.	What can your students do? (listen for response) What could be our next steps to get them to this level? (listen for response) Let's plan something to try next week to support your students in reaching this goal.
This morning his mom emailed me. You won't believe what she said...	I can tell you're upset about this situation. Let's talk after school today. I would love to support you in dealing with this situation when we have more time to discuss it. Right now, we need to focus on our PLC goals for today.
Half of my class is at-risk. How will they ever...	Let's look at their data that shows they are at-risk. What specific gaps do they have? (listen for response) Let's start with planning intervention. We can plan intentional small group lessons and interventions that will support your students in filling their gaps and scaffold their learning to meet the level of this student expectation.
The curriculum is horrible. I can't teach my students like this	Are your students showing specific gaps in learning their standards? What do you feel is not working? (listen for response) Let's look at your schedule and content to see where we can support students with these skills.
Did you see that email? Can you believe we have to do (...) now?	I have not seen the email. Can we discuss it after school? I'll take time to look at it later. If there is anything I can do to support you with this, I would love to. Today we are talking about (fill in PLC focus for the day).

Think through some conversations that could take place with your teachers. Preplan some responses here.

When you have a focus for your teams and designate someone to hold the team accountable, it helps the team maximize their work time during PLCs. As I began coaching PLCs, I watched the way my teams interacted. I learned their strengths as a team. I figured out which role each team member should play based on their strengths. This included my administration and me. We created some role clarity of who was responsible for what. You can see these different assignments in my sample digital PLC binder using the Resources QR code. On some teams, I was the leader of the PLC, on others, it was the team leader. In some PLCs I spoke the most. Sometimes, my Assistant Principal or Principal did the talking. It depended on the team and the purpose of the PLC. We were very intentional with our roles and the messages we conveyed.

Once you have identified each team member's role and created an environment focused on students, you need to focus on the work. I believe that more work will get done if more structure is provided to the PLC. To do this, you must have agreement from all parties involved. The teachers and admin must take equal ownership of the PLC. If one part of the team is not pulling their weight, the PLC will fail. Believe me, I've seen it. It's hard to do all the parts yourself, you need a willing and collaborative team. I've put together some tips to keep the team on track and focused on the goal.

- **Set Team Guidelines:** In an effort to give your team structure, I recommend creating team–collaborative norms, goals, and jobs. If you can individualize this for each team, you will get more personal buy–in. You could also do this as a campus, depending on the goals of your school or district. These first steps will help you build an efficient team with self–created expectations. I used the team–created guidelines to redirect the team when needed. Refer to the Coaching Toolkit to find a sample team digital notebook for PLCs and a Rubric from Solution Tree to assess your PLC team. Both can be found through the Resources QR code.

- **Post PLC Questions:** Anywhere and everywhere. On agendas, on the wall, on your door. The team needs to remember the priority questions when working within the PLC. Popularized by Rick DuFour (2006), the four critical questions of a PLC include:

  o What do we want all students to know and to be able to do?

  o How will be know if they learn it?

  o How will we respond when some students do not learn?

  o How will we extend the learning for students who are already proficient?

- **Create agendas:** This could be your role or a team member's role. Either way, it's important to focus on the work. I recommend sending agendas out ahead of time. If each team member knows their role for the meeting, knows the expectations of the work time, they can come prepared. There is nothing worse than a team coming to PLCs unprepared. Talk about a time waster! Outline specific tasks and the amount of time you'll spend on each task. List the end–of–session goals, materials to bring, and questions to consider for the work time. Refer to the QR code to access a sample agenda.

- **Set Goals:** While each teacher, most likely, has their own professional goal which opens great opportunities for coaching, the PLC team should also have a goal. A more effective PLC will keep one to two goals at the forefront of their work. When PLCs turn into just another meeting or training, teams lose interest and focus. The work is no longer efficient or effective. By prioritizing one or two goals, the team can stay focused on the work, and the PLC process becomes an ongoing cycle that happens all year long.

Here are some sample PLC goals:

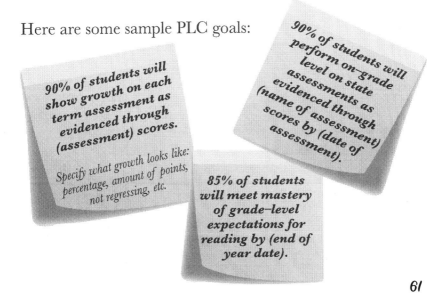

90% of students will show growth on each term assessment as evidenced through (assessment) scores.

Specify what growth looks like: percentage, amount of points, not regressing, etc.

90% of students will perform on-grade level on state assessments as evidenced through (name of assessment) scores by (date of assessment).

85% of students will meet mastery of grade–level expectations for reading by (end of year date).

Using goals like these, you can streamline your PLC work for the year. PLC sessions will look different depending on the work at hand, however, the cycle will focus on one ultimate goal.

What are some goals your PLC teams could work towards?

Structure & Choice

The most difficult PLC team I worked with always seemed to find a way to get off on a tangent. No matter how much I tried to redirect the conversation or look to leadership to handle the situation, the teachers found a way to answer questions with questions, keeping us in a spiral of confusion and frustration. It seemed like we never got anywhere in PLC meetings, and every time the team left at the end of the meeting I felt defeated. I felt like my head was caught in a whirlwind, and I didn't know up from down.

What I came to learn is that this team needed clear expectations, structures, and a voice. They needed to know ahead of time what we would focus on during the meeting and what our goal would be for the day. They needed an outlet to post their other questions and concerns and know they would be answered later. They had a strong voice that needed to be heard, and they wanted all concerns to be addressed. Giving them structure and a voice in their PLC meetings helped us get back on track. It helped us make the most of our time and, although they may not have left each PLC with something in–hand, they left with new knowledge. We had hard, much–needed conversations and problem–solved issues. Then, they implemented their solutions, in their own way, back in the classroom. All they wanted was someone to listen to their issues and affirm their thinking. Once they felt secure in the solutions they created, the team went above and beyond to meet administrators' expectations and improve student learning.

I have strong convictions that teachers need structure and choice within a PLC. They need to have their voice heard and an opportunity to complete tasks that are most important to them. The PLC cycle simply follows the pattern of analyzing data, planning for instruction, implementing the plan, reflecting, and adjusting. Because the PLC is a continuous cycle that includes many different moving parts, each session can look different. But all PLCs should be focused on the priority goal. I suggest giving teachers a visual or a list of options for PLC activities based on the type of work they will be doing. In the past, I've used menus based on content areas to provide teacher choices. There is a menu attached to the Coaching Toolkit through the Resources QR code. Here are some suggestions based on the cycle component.

Cycle Phase:	Suggestions:
Analyzing Data	Student Performance: • How are our at–risk students performing? • Are all student groups performing the same?
Analyzing Data	Question/Skill Analysis: • What trends do we see in skill strengths and weaknesses? • What misconceptions do our students have? • What skills were taught well? Which skills need reteaching?

Planning Instruction	Create/Plan any of the following based on immediate need seen in data: • Small group plans • Differentiation opportunities • Intervention plans • Reteach lessons • Spiral activities • Exit tickets, re–assessments • Extension activities
Learning	Engage teachers in modes of learning, such as: • Research and reflection • Article analysis • Mini PD session • Instructional Rounds • Video learning
Implementation & Reflection	Analyze and reflect on artifacts. Artifacts could include: • Student samples • Exit tickets • Lesson notes • Observational data
Monitor & Adjust	Adjust components of instruction based on data: • Lesson plans • Small groups • Intervention Groups • Extension activities

Each phase of the PLC cycle is important to the progress of teacher development and student growth. The phases can vary in the amount of time it takes to complete the work depending on the goal of the session. Knowing and understanding the expectations of your district, campus or administrators of how PLCs will be implemented is important. PLCs might be scheduled weekly, bi–weekly, monthly, after school, during conferences, or half–days with subs. It really depends on the administrator's expectations. Once you know the scope of what PLCs will look like, you can decide how much time and how many sessions you will spend within each phase.

The planning and learning phases will usually take the longest. Learning may need to happen before planning, or vice versa, depending on the skillset of your teachers and what the data is showing the team. The area of growth presented by the data may be an opportunity for teachers to learn and grow which will require some specific learning activities in PLCs to help them prepare for planning instruction.

Learning may happen after a plan is implemented. A team may know specifically what needs to be done, only to hit a roadblock along the way. This will provide an opportunity to assess the situation and find ways to overcome the roadblock. Through this process, there will be learning involved.

To ensure time is not wasted during the different phases, always come prepared. During each phase think about implementing structures to keep the team on task and focused. During the data analysis phase, I recommend preparing the data ahead of time to reflect on the specific concerns you or your administration have identified. Bring pre–planned questions to help guide the analysis of the data and the conversation about the data. This gives teachers the opportunity to discover what the data is showing them in turn guiding them in the direction you have identified as the biggest need.

Before ending the Data Analysis phase, ask the team to write their goals for the planning or learning phase depending on what the team needs at that time. Use this to hold them accountable for your next PLC session. Encourage the teams to identify, specifically, what materials, support, and goals they have for their next session. Having these items identified before the next PLC session will help the team use their time efficiently in the next phase. I always tried to remind my team ahead of time what the topic of the next PLC was and what materials they needed to bring. Being prepared saves time.

You might begin to notice that the last four phases of the cycle may interweave, and that's OK! Constantly implementing, reflecting, monitoring and adjusting is necessary for good teaching. Instead of thinking of the PLC cycle as a cycle, think of it as an ongoing, interwoven process. Also know that you or an administrator needs to consistently provide guidance and structure to these PLC sessions to keep the work moving forward.

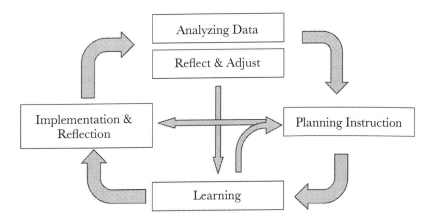

Take a minute to reflect on the traditional PLC Cycle and my version of the PLC Cycle. How does this change your thinking about how you will structure PLCs within your school or district?

Well–Oiled Machines

There are times when you will encounter some well–oiled machines, aka efficient, hard–working teams. These teams can function on their own in a PLC. They don't need your guidance or structures. They have it together. These are the most amazing teams. You know no matter what the task, they will get it done. When you have teams like this, your approach must be very different. You do not want to squash their independence and functionality. If this is the case, I suggest letting the teams work on their own with you as an observer. While you probably don't need to prioritize being in their PLCs, drop in when you can to listen, observe, and share ideas.

I recommend still holding these teams accountable, but allow them to provide their own agendas, structures, and systems. Either you or the administration need to know what they are working on. Ask these teams to turn in things like agendas, artifacts, or goals. Knowing their focus helps you provide support and learning opportunities, when needed. They will most likely come to you when they need the support and you will be ready with ideas if you're kept in the loop.

The easiest way to think about intervening with teams is thinking about instruction as a classroom teacher. The ones who struggle more will need more support. Those that struggle less will need less support. You can implement a gradual release model with your PLC team. Begin by directly leading components at first, then gradually release the process to the team through guided practice and independent practice. Continue to provide opportunities for discussion, collaboration, and choice to give teams ownership of the PLC. Just know you may be doing more of the work for some time until the team becomes more efficient. This would also be a good time to lean on your administration to split up the work and roles and share the responsibility of guiding each PLC team.

Reflections & Takeaways

Coaching with Style

Finally! Let's talk *coaching*. I bet you thought we would never get to this point. I think of coaching much like I do instruction. There is a framework to follow, but we also have to meet the needs of the individuals we are working with. Building relationships and differentiating for learners are important components to a successful partnership between a coach and teacher. When you understand the teacher's ability level and willingness to learn, you can modify your coaching style to meet their individual needs. The choices you make throughout the coaching cycle will contribute to the success of the coaching partnership and the growth of the teacher.

One Size Fits None

The Jim Knight Framework (2017) coaching cycle includes: **Identify** > **Learn** > **Improve**. Although the Identify stage can be intimidating to teachers at times, the

Learning stage is probably the most vulnerable stage in the coaching cycle. This is the phase where you are truly *coaching*. One thing that took me a while to perfect was my coaching style. Teachers need differentiated instruction and multiple access points within their learning just like students. They need to be met where they are and be given options to choose their method of instruction. My advice would be to give your teachers choices. *How would they like to be coached?*

I've developed many coaching styles from various resources that I have shared with my teachers. There are many different ways you can allow teachers to communicate their coaching preferences with you. Some methods you can use are surveys, forms, coaching conversations, or menus to communicate your coaching options. Find the method that works best for you and your staff. Be flexible with your method as well. Year to year, you may notice that different methods work better or worse than they did the year before. Always be willing to monitor and adjust your coaching tools, methods, and strategies to best meet the needs of your staff.

If you are a newer coach, I recommend trying three or four of the coaching styles below and add in more year after year. This gives you time to perfect a coaching style and make it your own. It will allow you time to find your niche and create your own coaching styles. Here's the list I have built over my years of coaching. Feel free to steal, tweak, adjust and use.

Coaching Styles

 Model & Debrief

Modeling and debriefing is a great opportunity to teach multiple teachers at the same time. It is also useful for teams who have set goals together. This structure can be used during PLCs. I would model a skill while the teachers played the part of the students. After the model, we would debrief about what they saw and discuss ways they could implement the practice in their classroom. Together we would make a plan. The teachers would then implement the strategy or skill throughout the week. At the next PLC we would discuss how the implementation went.

 Whisper–In

This is helpful when teachers want immediate feedback. In this structure, the coach observes a teacher during the instructional time or activity of which they have requested feedback. As the teacher is teaching, the coach has the opportunity to whisper–in feedback directly in the moment to support their practice.

 Watch & Learn

During Watch & Learn, the coach models a lesson in the classroom. The teacher watches and takes notes during the lesson to grow within their practice. It's always a good idea to debrief and answer any questions the teacher has after modeling the lesson. It's also a good time to share with the teacher any adjustments you would personally make to your lesson based on how it went in the classroom. This models a reflective practice for teachers and gives them a voice in the process.

 ## Copycat

The Copycat structure is perfect for teachers who are fairly strong and teach multiple rotations. In this structure, the coach models a lesson during a rotation while the teacher observes and takes notes. During the following rotations, the teacher teaches the lesson on their own, copying what they have just witnessed. Variations of this could include the coach staying for the second rotation and offering feedback through a co–teach model or whisper–in. If a conference period falls within rotations, the coach and the teacher could debrief before the teacher copies the lesson on their own. I typically provide all materials for all of the following rotations. That way, the teacher has all the materials ready for the next rotation.

 ## Co–Teach

Co–Teach is a more common structure of coaching. The coach and teacher plan a lesson together and co–teach the lesson in the classroom. This is a good opportunity for the teacher to use their strengths while the coach supplements the instruction with additional instructional methods.

 Voice Over

Voice Over is another form of modeling. During Voice Over, the coach interrupts their modeling to voice–over or share information about what they are implementing. This could be background information, specific teacher moves, something they noticed about the students, etc. This structure is useful to help teachers understand the reasons behind the instructional practice. They can see the how, why, and when of implementing the practice.

 Video Share

The Video Share structure is just like it sounds! The teacher records a video of themselves and shares the video with the coach. Together they look for areas of improvement and make a plan.

 Video Reflect

Video Reflect is geared towards strong teachers who are motivated to self–reflect and improve. Teachers with a growth mindset benefit from this coaching option. The teacher records themselves and reflects independently on the video looking for areas of improvement. Often, teachers will then ask a coach for some assistance but not always. I suggest using a form of completion for this structure as a way to provide accountability and keep you informed of the teacher's personal growth. You will find a sample video reflection form in the Coaching Toolkit.

 ## Hands–Together

Hands–Together is an ideal structure to use with strong teachers or teachers who just need some support planning. With this structure, a coach offers support to help a teacher plan an assessment, lesson, or activity. The coach offers an outside viewpoint to the planning. This is a great opportunity to remind teachers of the most important aspect of planning: the students' needs. This collaborative planning session will support teachers in trying new strategies, allow them to consider different ways of thinking, and allow them to reflect on their current practice.

 ## Sounding Board

Sometimes, great teachers just need someone to be their sounding board. Why not offer that as a coaching structure? In this structure, teachers set a meeting with you just to brainstorm or process ideas. It offers them immediate feedback in order to move forward with the planning or implementation process. This structure can be used during PLC meetings or individual meetings. One of my best 5th grade teachers (who eventually became a coach) gave me this idea. She just needed someone to listen to her ideas and tell her she wasn't crazy. She was innovative and self–motivated. All she needed was me as a sounding board to help her process and plan out her ideas. It was the ideal situation for a highly qualified teacher.

To reflect on these coaching styles further, consider the ability of the teacher and the level of support they need. The message sent with these coaching strategies is important. If you are doing more of the work, such as modeling, the message should be: *Exemplars provide conceptual understanding.* This tells teachers that, in this case, you are the expert giving them a model example.

MODEL	Strategies
You: Give an example in action.	Video or Live
Them: Observe & learn.	Chunking/MicroPD
Message: Exemplars provide conceptual understanding.	Copy-cat

If the work is shared, such as co–teaching, the message should be: *Collaboration brings growth for all.* This tells teachers that you are willing to learn alongside them, and together you can achieve greatness.

PARTNER	Strategies
You: Listen, guide, provide. **Them**: Think, share, reflect. **Message**: Col-LABOR-ation brings growth for all.	🤝 Hands-Together 🔊))) Sounding board 👥 Co-teach

If the teacher is in a space to receive feedback in action, such as you watching them teach, the message should be: It's OK to try. It's OK to fail. Progress is worth more than perfection. This tells the teacher that you are supporting them in taking risks. You'll be there to guide them along the way, and there is no judgment.

SHADOW	Strategies
You: Observe, learn, support. **Them**: Practice live! **Message**: It's OK to try. It's OK to fail. Progress over perfection.	💬 Whisper-In ✏️ Watch & Learn

Think about your teachers. Which coaching strategy would work best for your individual teachers? Which ones do you think they might prefer?

Build Connections

With these structures I have just shared with you, there are some that are more directive and some that are more collaborative. Within all of these, you still want to give the teachers some voice and choice. The key is to find where those pieces lay. The great thing about providing a variation of the coaching structures is that you can meet each teacher's individual needs and learning style. You probably noticed that some structures are geared towards those who need explicit explanation and some are geared towards those who just need an outsider's view.

When you give choice in your coaching style, the teachers who need the most help may not pick the structure that would best support them. That is OK! Start small; build the relationship and give it time. When you start small and build their trust in you, they will try a different structure that seems more of a risk to them. Think of a trust fall. Some may not be willing to go all the way at the beginning. They may need to take small steps first. They may fall two inches, then increase to five. Then, a foot. Then, four feet. Just give it time and continue to support them in the best way you can until they, finally, go all the way.

With one of my most challenging teachers, I think my "in" was helping her talk to a parent. She had a significant amount of data to support her case but was terrified of how the parent would react to her concerns. I sat with her and led the conversation with the parent, explaining all of the data, and offering our educational suggestions to the parent. The meeting went very well. The teacher was pleased and, finally, came to trust me. After that, we went on to work together. Little by little, we created lessons, activities, and assessments. I happened to be more tech savvy than she was, and any way I could support her with technology was another in. She began to appreciate the amount of time I spent with her working on these items. Within three years, I was her go–to person. You may be thinking, *three years*?! Yes, some relationships take that much time. Although that was definitely one of my hardest relationships to build, it was worth it.

Other relationships you will want to spend time building are those that show strengths in their teaching practice. These are the teachers that usually have a good reputation around the school and can vouch for you with the staff. These are usually the teachers with a growth mindset who will be willing to work with you and will need a less directive mode of coaching. Build those connections as well, they will come in handy when you need the extra help and support!

When other teachers start hearing about the cool and innovative ideas you have planned with these strong teachers, they will begin to see your worth. They will begin to buy–in to the idea of coaching and will come to you for help. These are the connections you want to build. You want to build trust, confidence, and curiosity. When other teachers begin to believe that you are good at what you do and trust that you have their best interests at heart, they will be curious about how you can help them too. This is the place you want to be. So, use your strong teachers to build your reputation.

Dialogue & Voice

There are many reasons why a teacher might be reluctant to have a coach. It could be pride or insecurity. It could be personal. I've worked with them all. It is important to get to know your teachers. Talking with them and listening to them will give you insight into their personality. If you learn how they feel about themselves and how they feel about teaching, you can find ways to intervene. Listen for the hidden messages, or ask them flat out. Just take the time to get to know them.

"When we aren't curious in conversations we judge, tell, blame and even shame, often without even knowing it, which leads to conflict."

~Kirsten Siggins

Some teachers will still continue to reject your help. Don't take it personally. Ninety–nine percent of the time, it has nothing to do with you. Usually, there is some underlying issue that you know nothing about. You cannot control these types of situations. Let it go. Forcing yourself on the teacher will only hinder the relationship from ever being built. Ultimately, they will come around. Invest the time to build the relationship through each minor encounter. Show you respect them through a smile or a hello in the hall. Drop them a note to praise a strength you've observed, personal or professional. You can even just say, *"I noticed your haircut, it's super cute."* Just show them you are here and available in any way possible. This will begin to build a rapport with the teacher. Eventually, they will talk to you more. When they do, listen. Listen with your heart.

Give them the opportunity to dialogue and have their voice heard. At some point, they will need help, and they will turn to you because you have built their trust.

In some cases, you may not have the option to remove yourself from the situation, and take the time to slowly build the relationship. Maybe you have been directed to work with this reluctant teacher and they feel forced to work with you. This is not going to help your relationship with them. In this case, my suggestion is to kill them with kindness and continue to push forward. Open dialogue to discuss the working relationship. What are their expectations for working with you? What are their goals for the work you will do together? Create some clarity for your role as their coach and some clarity for them as the teacher. As you create clarity, here are a few things you could remind them of:

- You are not their administrator.
- You are not their evaluator.
- You don't have all the answers.
- Your job is to support them.
- You will do it together.

Again, the more you can dialogue with a teacher and let their voice be heard, the more they will trust you. All any teacher wants is to be heard and valued. If you can show them this, then they will trust you to be their coach.

Earlier we talked about these reluctant teachers and some strategies for pushing out new initiatives. Here is a list of suggested ways to deal with these teachers and to gain their trust in YOU as their coach.

Skeptical	Resistant	Insecure
Impress with your knowledge & expertise	Kill with kindness	Scaffold their learning to build success
Use testimonials from other teachers	Do small favors to build trust	Differentiate your expectations
Model how you would like to be treated	Show your worth by sharing testimonials or data from other successful coaching partnerships	Use a gradual release model of coaching
Praise, Praise, Praise!	Praise, Praise, Praise!	Praise, Praise, Praise!

Take a minute to reflect. Make a list of specific actions you could take to build relationships with skeptical, resistant or insecure teachers? What will be your next steps?

Virtual Coach

Many of you may be living in a world where coaching has become virtual. COVID closures and new technology have adapted the way coaching can work. If you're currently in a role that requires you to coach from afar, I want to let you know that it is still possible. In fact, in–person coaches could probably take some tips from remote coaches. It may be harder to build initial relationships in this kind of position, but it is attainable. It is important to take time upfront to get to know the teacher you are coaching. I recommend spending the first coaching meeting getting to know the teacher. You might ask them to reflect on their strengths and weaknesses, successes and challenges. Just give them time to talk and you to listen. Take notes if needed to remember details about the teacher. This can serve as a helpful tool; refer back to your notes before coaching meetings to remember these details. Until you really get to know the teacher, you can use your notes as talking points to build connections and check in on them throughout the process. Through the Resources QR code, you'll find a sample note–taking document to learn about your teachers during your initial meeting.

Although creating and maintaining relationships may be a little more difficult, the advantage of remote coaching is time efficiency and direct coaching impact. In this role, I found that the easiest way to impact a teacher is through video recording. Many teachers that receive in–person coaching hesitate when it comes to video recording, but virtual coaching makes it a necessity. When a teacher video records a lesson, it makes the coaching very direct and data–driven. In your first meeting with the teacher, you'll probably identify a challenge or goal that currently exists. Use this as leverage for your partnership. Ask the teacher to videotape the portion of instructional time that is reflected in their goal or challenge. To keep the partnership time efficient, watch the video ahead of time, make notes, collect data, and create a presentation slide. During the meeting, I spend time praising the teacher, sharing things I noticed and asking questions. I then drive the conversation to an actionable goal. This leads to the next video, and the cycle continues until the practice is perfected and it's time for a new goal. This is very efficient coaching!

I believe in–person coaches could mimic the same format with a video recording platform using a flipped coaching model. Teachers would submit videos, then schedule their coaching meeting. The coaching meeting can be anywhere from 15 to 45 minutes depending on the amount of discussion and practice that needs to happen in relation to the actionable goal. If you can keep the meeting succinct, then you can protect the teacher's time to work on other duties. They will definitely appreciate this!

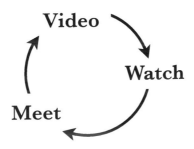

Using a model like this forces a coach to pick small, attainable goals that can happen immediately in the next lesson that is recorded. These small steps help keep teachers from feeling overwhelmed and allows them to feel immediate success. This is also a great way to expose teachers to a multitude of instructional practices. Set a primary purpose, then identify small goals within the overarching goal as you progress through the coaching relationship. For example, the overarching goal might be increased engagement. Within that goal, you may coach the teacher on using active response structures to get students engaged (chanting, polling, sticky notes, whiteboards). Then, you might coach the teacher on increasing student talk to engage students (A/B Partners, Elbow Partners, or Round Robin Share). Each structure will take one session to teach and practice. Then the teacher can immediately implement the structure in their next lesson. As you expose them to more and more instructional practices, the teachers fill their teaching tool box with all kinds of tools!

Reflections & Takeaways

Gentle Accountability

> *"We don't have to be the fidelity police. We just have to provide freaking awesome support."*
>
> ~Jim Knight

I love this quote by Jim Knight. Our job as a coach is not to be the accountability police, but we can be the influencers. Influencers can guide teachers in the right direction by providing the best support possible. If you remember, some of the best advice I received from an administrator was to always respond, *"How can I help you with that goal/task/etc.?"* Although we can't change the initiatives or give teachers permission to not follow them, we can provide support. Ultimately, it is your administrator that must hold their feet to the fire. It's also a decision that an administrator must make to support these initiatives. They need to have full investment as well to ensure the success of any directive from themselves or the administration above them.

While I was an instructional coach in my last district, we went through a big curriculum change. Many teachers opposed the change. It was a long journey to get them on board. I know some teachers are still skeptical about the curriculum today. You won't always be able to convince everyone that change is best, but there are strategies you can use, as a coach, to help you influence people to follow the given expectations.

Know Your Teachers

First and foremost, as I've stated many times already, you must know your teachers. When you really know your teachers, you'll know who will oppose the change and who will immediately jump on board. You'll know who needs to see it to believe it or who needs to read about it to understand it. This will only happen when you have relationships established. Just as a teacher understands their students' learning styles and what helps them become successful, as a coach, you need to discover your teachers' learning styles and what will make them successful.

If you're new to your role and you haven't had time to build relationships, I would try a variety of each of the strategies that follow. Spread your net wide, in hopes to grasp them all. Through the journey, remember to be your authentic self. Teachers respond better to honesty and vulnerability. Sometimes it's hard to push a directive when you don't even understand it yourself. When you have no experience with it, haven't read the research, haven't seen it in action, it's hard to convince people that you know what you're talking about. Don't try to pretend. Remind teachers you are learning and growing with them; you will tackle this new adventure together.

Find the Why

I always started with the WHY. As naive as people may think I am, I've always been a believer. You give me a reason to believe it, and I will. So, I always start with logic. *Why has our district, campus, or principal decided to make this change and push out this mandate?* There is always a reason why, and often, it is a reason bigger than one teacher and their classroom. Sometimes, this is hard for teachers to grasp. They may only see their students and their class. They may not realize there is always a bigger agenda when running a campus or district. Usually, the change stems from district or campus data; present this to teachers.

Our district transition, at the time, was focused on the amount of students not making progress in reading in our Kindergarten through 3rd grade classes. The gaps our district leaders found in the data showed students were not mastering the necessary skills by third grade to prepare for state assessments. When I presented this data, I found that some teachers responded with a sense of urgency to try something new and see if they could help close the gaps. Others opposed the idea of change. They felt their students had consistently performed well; why change? In this situation, you could take a couple of different routes. Consider your relationship with the teacher to decide which route to take.

The first choice is to dig deeper into the data to see if their students stayed consistently successful in reading in the years following. If students were not continually successful, you could show the data to that teacher and explain how students could have been successful in their class at that time, but the learning didn't stick. Make a case for aligning instruction throughout all grade levels to help make the learning transfer from each grade level to the next.

The second choice is to dig deeper into the teacher's specific instructional strategies. Point out that their students are successful because they have already implemented many of the components of the new initiative. Use this teacher as a leader to help with the change. You can have them model the strategies they use for other teachers. Let them lead a PLC or training. Have the teacher bring student artifacts and explain their instructional practices.

Either of these choices may help a reluctant teacher change their opinion of new expectations or practices. If neither of these work or the teacher doesn't fit into either of these categories, continue with a different strategy.

Present the Research

Some teachers thrive on numbers. They love data, and they just need to see the research. Once they can see the numbers, they will jump on board. However, some may not be data–driven, but when they see the research, they may begin to consider the idea of change.

Our new curriculum had a good amount of research to support it, but it was still a hard transition for many teachers. It was a completely new way of teaching for them. In this case, you may need to present some examples of what it looks like in conjunction with the research. Videos and modeling are very helpful in this situation. In the past, I have led professional development opportunities with an article analysis activity where teachers read an article and used a specific protocol to analyze their reading. I intentionally used protocols and driving questions to guide their thinking in the ideal direction. Then, I would follow up with a discussion structure and video. This gives teachers time to process what they have read, build connections through discussion, and visualize the article they read earlier. Oftentimes, through this process, teachers will realize they can do what we are asking. It's not that hard. It makes it real for them and more attainable.

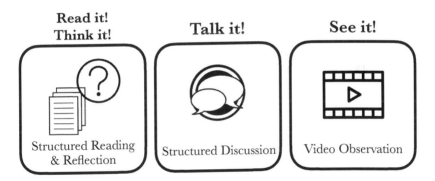

Read it! Think it! — Structured Reading & Reflection

Talk it! — Structured Discussion

See it! — Video Observation

Flexibility Not Fidelity

Another way to make reform efforts more attainable is to help them see where the flexibility lies. I have a love–hate relationship with the word *fidelity*. Honestly, I probably hate it more than I love it. Teachers hate it too. It gives off a feeling of restriction. Teachers are creative, self–driven human beings. They like to have control. They like to have a choice. They do not like to be told, "You must do it this way."

That being said, I wholeheartedly agree that some programs will fail if they are not *routinely*, *consistently*, and *intentionally* implemented. This is why we need to help teachers see the flexibility. Most programs have a purpose and structure. Help teachers identify the purpose and understand the structures in order to implement it with *intentionality*. Once teachers can see the purpose, understand the structure, and see how it fits with their current practice, they can create their personal style around the new expectations.

This is a fine line to monitor and control as a coach. You must be very observant as you begin to collaborate with teachers on how to implement the new expectations with their own flair. Be very direct on what parts are non–negotiable and which parts have room for adjustment. Start with the choices. Show teachers different variations of those options to see where the flexibility lies, but model it without losing the *intention* of the directive.

In our curriculum change, the interactive read–aloud was an area that teachers could adjust. They could use their personal preferences to choose a text that they enjoyed. Teachers were encouraged to think about texts that their class would enjoy and connect with. Teachers also had the option to select what skills they would emphasize during the read–aloud. This was a great opportunity to introduce new skills, spiral skills already taught, practice communication and collaboration, or instill reflection and independent thinking. It was really up to the teacher how they structured their read–aloud for the day. What was not optional? Eliminating the read–aloud from the Reader's Workshop block or using texts that were not developmentally or age–appropriate.

With this in mind, I often used PLCs to dissect the standards within each unit. As a team, we would collaborate to decide which skills and texts we would use during the Interactive Read Aloud (IRA) portion of the Reader's Workshop. We would map out the unit on a collaborative document for the whole team. Teachers could then individually decide if they wanted to use stop and jots, turn and talks, reflection journals, etc. to practice skills being taught within the IRA. They could use their own style to create anchor charts, implement discussion, and so on. Each teacher had the chance to share their voice throughout the process and show their creative style as a teacher.

I always try to remember Todd Whitaker's message about curriculums and programs: it's not programs that work, it's teachers. Any skilled teacher can make any program successful. Any unskilled teacher can make any program fail. When considering these statements, think about your strongest teachers and weakest teachers. Think about who would help support the new program and who would not. This will drive how you strategically show the successes of the program. Who will be your model classroom? Who will help lead trainings and meetings? These are the teachers you need to lean on through this process.

Bring in the Cheerleaders

When you have identified your strong teachers and you have their support, use them to build positivity throughout the campus. Use their stories and examples to share with the staff. Build collaboration between them and other teachers.

Remember back in school when we wanted to be popular? We wanted to do what the cool kids were doing. Use that! Make it cool to "try the new." Peer pressure can work! If you keep showing the naysayers the great things happening in other classrooms and with other students, they may change their tune. Sometimes they just need to be a follower, not a leader. They need someone to pave the way. They need to see it in action and witness the results. Use your out–going, positive, strong teachers to pave that way. This also gives those strong teachers an opportunity to build their leadership skills. It helps them build a resume for their future. They may have dreams of becoming an instructional coach, assistant principal, or principal one day. Let them begin to develop those skills as a leader! You can't manage change on your own, you need support too! Let these strong teachers support you and help you through this transition.

Embrace with Grace

The last suggestion I have, in an effort to influence teachers in following any expectations, directives or mandates, is to fully embrace it yourself. You must model an attitude of embracing your administration's wishes for teachers. People are easily influenced by watching and listening to others. Once, at a convocation ceremony, a speaker shared his story of being a positive force in the community. His message told a story of how we, as educators, create the image that the community sees by the way we act and speak. If we're complaining about the school system, administrators, or students, then we are sending a message of negativity about education. In turn, people in the community lose respect for our educational entity. This message resonated with me when I first heard it. Additionally, this may even be an unintentional message we send. Once, my grandfather asked me if I like my job. I responded with *Of course!* I was confused as to why he would ask. He pointed out that most of my social media posts included Sunday dramatics about having to go to work on Monday. Wednesday posts about joyfully making it to hump day and counting down the rest of the week; and Friday posts about how excited I was for the weekend. To him, the message I was sending was that I was counting down to the weekend with a lack of passion for my job. This was not the message I wanted to send.

Both of these instances really made me think about the way I act and the things I say in reference to education. We create the image we want people to see by the way we act and speak. If you want the community to think positively about your school, then you should speak positively about your school in public. If you want people to think positively about education and teachers, then you should speak positively about education and teachers in the community. This is the same concept. To have teachers buy–in and believe in change, YOU must speak and act positively about the change presented.

As you are embracing the newness, you can, gently, hold teachers and teams accountable using collaboration and planning. Lead with grace, and guide the work towards the goal. This can happen during PLCs, meetings, discussions, or through emails. Strategically planning professional development, PLCs, and staff meetings can support administration in accomplishing their goals. Always consider the teachers' feelings and opinions as you plan these learning opportunities. By giving them a voice through collaboration, they will feel involved in the process. Making teachers a priority in the planning will allow them to take ownership of HOW the change will happen. Here are some suggestions of how you can collaborate with teachers to implement a change.

- *Create a timeline of implementation, outlining goals for each step.*

- *Design "Look Fors." What will it look like in action?*

- *Teacher leaders model various components for team(s).*

- *Collaborative discussions to problem-solve concerns.*

Along with incorporating teachers into the process, you can influence the trajectory of the implementation of the initiative by providing reminders and support along the way. This may need to be individualized coaching for specific teachers. It could involve celebrations for hitting specific targets or goals throughout the process. You might send out weekly tips or reminders to keep the staff focused on the goal. Newsletters could provide additional professional learning opportunities offered by you or independent tasks that teachers can participate in to monitor their own learning and understanding. However you decide to provide support to teachers along the way, remember to always have a growth mindset and continue to follow–up. If you get off track from the goal or stop putting it at the forefront of everything you do, it will lose momentum. Teachers will see the opportunity to jump ship. They will think it's just another education fad that will go away. Stay the course!

Slow and Steady, Wins the Race

I want to be clear that change doesn't happen overnight. Sometimes, this can be hard for educators to grasp. Change takes time. Be patient with yourself and with your teachers. Set small targets that will keep you moving towards the end goal. Celebrate those successes. Remind

 yourself and your staff of where you started and how far you have come. You can do this with data or with testimonies from teachers. By using the Resources QR code, you will find a sample data walk form that I used for data tracking in classrooms. I created this form to prioritize our goals as a campus. Calculating the data collected from these forms gave me many opportunities to share percentages of growth in different components with teachers. It helped us set next steps as we moved towards our end goal. It held teachers accountable but also showed them their growth.

Thought—out, strategic implementation is the best way to carry out anything new. If you rush the process, you will lose people along the way. Step back and reflect. Be intentional. Consider all components involved, predict down—falls, and analyze the skill level of your staff. Create a plan and intentionally meet your goals, day by day.

Think about a challenge you have ahead of you. How can you break this down into purposeful steps? Create a timeline or outline of the projected targets.

Reflections & Takeaways

Managing It ALL

Prioritizing Time

Roles, responsibilities, relationships, REAL talk… It's a lot. How can we manage it all and not feel overwhelmed? It takes balance and priorities. First and foremost, you must decide what your *impact* will be, what your *goals* are as a coach, and where the majority of your *time* should be spent. While I believe that a coach's time should be spent coaching, that is not always what happens. Depending on your role, you may have other assigned duties: lunch duty, car duty, intervention, social committee, decorating committee. So, how do we re–focus our time on coaching? I created a realistic framework for myself to 1) affirm me in my role as a coach and 2) manage my time appropriately. Coaching encompasses many duties that must happen to impact teachers. I summarized these into three categories: Providing Exemplars, Gather & Disperse, Creating & Planning. Each of these areas could equally be split between 90% of your time. The other 10% can be delegated to other duties as assigned. Having this framework reminds me that all the tedious tasks I'm performing are directly related to coaching. It also helps me refocus my time when I am staying in that 10% too long!

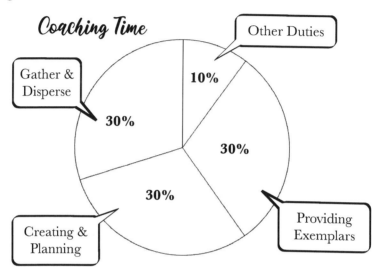

Providing Exemplars includes sharing exemplar instructional techniques with teachers. This includes any task related to teaching teachers by example.

Gather & Disperse encompasses tasks that are related to gathering information or dispersing information that directly correlates to your role as a coach. Anytime you're gathering information or sharing information would fall into this category.

Creating & Planning covers all the time it takes to plan and create the exemplars and instances of gathering and dispersing information.

Category Name:	Includes:
Providing Exemplars	Modeling in classrooms Teaching/Training teachers Planning with teachers
Gather & Disperse	Partnership Meetings Teacher Observations Continued Learning Opportunities Staff/District Communication
Creating & Planning	Creating and Planning for: • Modeling in classrooms • Leading learning opportunities • Meetings

You may be wondering how your time from 8am to 4pm will fit into this pie chart. How do you manage all the tasks in a timely fashion? My calendar was my best friend in hectic times. When I felt I couldn't manage it all, I had to sit down and plan out my time. Monthly and weekly, I processed what meetings I had coming up, what important dates and deadlines were approaching, and when all of my coaching would occur. I kept a large dry–erase board calendar in my office where I marked important dates monthly. This visual helped remind me of upcoming events that could take up a lot of my time. Using my personal digital calendar, I created time blocks to schedule all that needed to be accomplished each day. This might sound silly, but I literally set a daily appointment for checking emails. Adding items like these to my calendar reminded me that I had time available and I had to stay within that time limit. Like I said before, you don't want to get lost in all the day–to–day tasks. I prioritize my time on my calendar to reflect my priorities of coaching. Below is an example of my weekly calendar list. Setting aside time for specific tasks, kept me sane. I knew I would get to everything, and I had the time set aside to do it.

	Monday	Tuesday	Wednesday	Thursday	Friday
8 AM	Check Email	Check Email	Check Email	Check Email	Check Email
9 AM	Data Walks	Meet with Admin Leadership Team	Planning with Teachers	PLCs	Coaching Meetings
10 AM	PLC Planning				Creating Resources
11 AM	Model in Classrooms	Model in Classrooms			Planning for Upcoming PD Meetings
12 PM		Lunch Duty			
	Lunch	Lunch	Lunch	Lunch	Lunch
1 PM					
2 PM	Planning for Staff Meeting or Coaching Meetings	Data Walks	Planning with Teachers	PLCs	Coaching Meetings Creating Resources Planning for Upcoming PD Meetings
3 PM	Car Duty	Car Duty	Car Duty	Car Duty	Car Duty

The Art of Saying No

You're probably thinking, *What if I can't fit it all onto my calendar?!* Well, maybe you can't. That's OK, that's why we need to prioritize. Sometimes, you might have to say NO. As coaches, we are usually the go–getters, the dependable ones, the initiators. The administration will often call on us to help with extra tasks: lead this committee, attend that meeting, help create this item. Guess what? You don't have to do it all. Know your boundaries. In different seasons of life you may be able to take on more, but you may also have to take on less. You need to know your self–capacity and stick within a manageable range. Do not feel bad for saying no.

I often thought if I didn't do it, then it wouldn't get done. While this may have been true, a wise administrator told me one time, everyone is replaceable. As much as we may think that everything weighing on our shoulders is our responsibility, there are others out there just as talented and capable. Let someone else step in and take over. You don't have to do it all! You never know, it might be the opportunity another person needs to grow. You might actually be doing someone a favor by saying no. Creating boundaries for yourself is healthy. If we don't set limits to what we can manage, then we will become overwhelmed.

I was the type of coach that let everyone reach out to me whenever they wanted. This was fine, until I had kids. Then, I was a busy mom. I had to set limits on my communication with teachers after working hours. I had to set aside time in the evenings to be a mom. With that, I had to tell some people no. As my kids got older and became more self–sufficient, I relaxed my availability again. I became more apt to answer phone calls, texts, and emails late into the evening. Teachers became used to this convenience. Then, another season of life came along… COVID and family deaths. This was a very stressful time in my life, and I no longer had the emotional or mental capacity to handle every interaction with teachers as I had before. I had to learn to step away, turn my phone off, and ignore requests in order to gain back my capacity as an instructional leader. I had to prioritize. I spent more time with certain partnerships and less time with others. I focused on campus goals, not campus drama. I had to remove myself from situations where stress affected my work. I became hyper–focused on the necessary and disregarded the unnecessary. This separation allowed me to build back my emotional and mental capacity, eventually, returning to a season where, again, I was constantly available.

I definitely think my teachers saw this change in me. They were all respectful of my decisions, because we all have moments like this in life. We are human; life happens. We should all have grace to extend to another in a time of need. Be willing to extend grace, and others will be willing to extend it back.

Self–Reflection

In seasons of life that are difficult, it might be hard to see where your impact lies. It's important to remind yourself how far you have come, what you have accomplished, and refocus to find your next steps. As a coach, we have three goals: **Impact** people, **Improve** classroom instruction and **Increase** student success.

Periodically, we should take time to reflect on these areas in order to move forward. *How have you impacted people? How have you improved classroom instruction? How has students' success increased?* Count your successes, reflect on your misses, and move forward with new opportunities. Through the Resources QR code, you will find an Instructional Coach Reflection Checklist to guide you in analyzing your current reality of coaching.

Reflection brings progress. It's important to take a moment to STOP, BREATHE, REFLECT & RESUME. Through reflection, you'll find validation, affirmation, and inspiration. This is food for the soul and we all need this from time to time.

"Reflection... Looking back so the view looking forward is clearer."

~ *Unknown*

Self–Care

Outside of our coaching role, it is important to take care of ourselves. Our personal life affects our work life and vice versa. I believe it's important to set self–care goals. Just as students don't get the best if their teacher isn't feeling their best; our staff doesn't get our best, if we aren't feeling our best. It's important to take care of yourself. Think about what fuels you and set a goal that you can hold yourself accountable for, or reach out to another coach friend to check–in on you from time to time. My self–care goal is sleep. If I don't get enough sleep throughout the week, I'm a grumpy person. I need my beauty sleep to be the best version of me and not a curmudgeon.

Here are some strategies that you could use to refill yourself:

- **Find the Words:** Find a verse, quote or song that resonates with you and lifts you up. Read or listen to it when you need a moment to breathe and re–energize.

- **Time Away:** Schedule a date night or friends night. Take an evening all to yourself to enjoy good company, food, and laughter. Reconnect!

- **Relaxation:** What better way to relax than a hot, bubble bath? You may enjoy a hot tub or swimming pool or even just a glass of wine sitting on the back porch. Whatever it is, take a moment and do it. Relax!

- **Exercise:** Sometimes a walk, bike ride, or even a HIIT workout can help us relieve some stress. Take time to sweat it out and rejuvenate!

- **Read a Book/Listen to a Podcast:** One of my favorite ways to revitalize my soul is listening to a motivating educational podcast or reading a good educational book. Feed your educational soul with uplifting thoughts. Reignite your passion!

- **Guilty Pleasure:** Sometimes we just need to be brain dead for a little while! I love watching a guilty pleasure tv show or movie, just to forget the stress of my world and recharge.

- **Quality Time:** Part of my stress comes from thinking I don't do enough for my own kids. Take time to spend some quality time with each child at least once during the week. This one–on–one time will fill your heart and theirs! Reset!

- **Family First:** Think of a fun family activity that you could enjoy either during the week or on the weekend. We enjoy game nights. We play Guess Who?, Battleship or hide–and–seek. The kids love the games, and we get quality family time. Refocus!

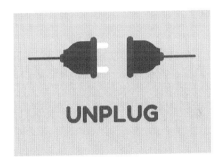

As you exercise self–care, remember to model this for your staff. It's beneficial to show them that you take time to reflect and balance your life. You might consider helping teachers set self–care goals as well. You can use these to check in on them from time to time. This builds relationships. These self–care plans will also be helpful in moments of frustration, burn–out, and distress. You can help teachers reflect on their self–care plan to see if they are refueling themselves to prevent emotions like these from happening.

> *"Almost everything will work again if you unplug it for a few minutes, including you."*
>
> ~*Anne Lamott*

Work, much like life, is about balance. Know when to say no, and when to take me-time. You can't do it all. We can't be perfect. We can only be authentically ourselves. Through reflection and self-care, we can be our best selves. We can prioritize our goals and respond with action. Our time and energy is precious. By prioritizing goals, protecting our time, and engaging in relationships, we can use our time and energy to impact those around us in the most profound ways.

Reflections & Takeaways

Final Thoughts

Coaching is much like teaching. There are good days and bad. Days you want to do over. Days you want to cry and go home, and days you want to shout from the mountain tops! Some teachers are easy to work with, some are hard. But it's all worth it in the end when you see their growth and the students' growth. Our job is not an easy one, but the reward is great. You are impacting humans. Children and adults watch you. They learn from you. Your school or district can become a better place because of you. Your work matters. On the hard days, keep pushing. Remember, it's for the kids. We all want our students to be able to have the best educational experience, and we can have an impact on that. Don't be hard on yourself or your teachers. Give yourself and them some grace. Lead with love, encourage with kindness, and push for change.

If it doesn't challenge you, it won't change you.

Acknowledgments

It takes a village to truly make you who you are.

Every interaction leaves a mark.

Every individual makes an impact.

My village molded me into the educator I am, and their impact guided my journey.

I would like to start by thanking my first principal, Steve Hudson, and his successor, Melinda Turner, for believing in me and providing me opportunities to learn and grow as a young educator. Mr. Hudson gave me my first opportunity at teaching. He guided me along my journey and bent over backward to support me as I grew as an educator. Mrs. Turner believed in me, trusted me, and gave me the opportunities to flourish.

I would like to thank Rhonda Nelson and Gabby Brown for mentoring me. Gabby took on the role of my mentor teacher during my first year of teaching and became a devoted friend. Rhonda taught me the ins and outs of working on curriculum. She supported me through my journey to gain my master's in curriculum and instruction and provided me opportunities to grow in my mathematical expertise.

A special thanks to my best friend, Crystal Shaklee, for continually pushing me to follow my ambitions, cheering me on along the way, and being that "teacher friend" that everyone needs in their life. Above everything else, Crystal, became the sister I never had, helped me find my way in my worst times and introduced me to the love of my life.

To my circle of administrative support: Megan Humphrey, Jennifer Penton, Katie Braden, Dr. Mary Johnston, and Dr. JJ Villareal, thank you for challenging me. Thank you for growing me, and thank you for trusting me.

To Becky Reidling, thank you for letting me coach. Thank you for providing me the opportunity to partner with teachers, build messy relationships, learn from my mistakes, and lead to the best of my ability.

The most important thank you, goes to the TEACHERS. All of those that I have worked with in–person and virtually, thank you for giving me the opportunity to partner with you. Each of you left an impact on me, and I hope I left an impact on you. Our interactions and friendships will never be forgotten. If you're reading this and think, *"Is she talking about me?"* I probably am. Know that you left a special mark on my heart.

Since leaving the campus environment I found a new group of supporters, my edupreneur group, and I would like to thank them all for their support, as well as, my publishers Darrin Peppard and Jessica Peppard for their guidance throughout this journey. This wouldn't be possible without them.

You all are My Village. My Community. My People. And I want to say Thank You.

"The greatness of a community is most accurately measured by the compassionate actions of its members."

~Coretta Scott King

References

5 whys: The ultimate root cause analysis tool. Kanban Software for Agile Project Management. (n.d.). Retrieved September 1, 2022, from https://kanbanize.com/lean–management/improvement/5–whys–analysis–tool

Covey, S. R. (2020). *7 Habits of highly effective people.* SIMON & SCHUSTER LTD.

DuFour, R., DuFour, R., Eaker, R., & Many, T. (2006). *Learning by Doing: A Handbook for Professional Learning Communities at Work.* Solution Tree.

Fay, J., & Fay, C. (2010). *Teaching with love and logic: Taking control of the classroom.* Love and Logic Institute, Inc.

Garmston, R. J., & Zimmerman, D. P. (2013). *Lemons to Lemonade: Resolving problems in meetings, workshops and plcs.* Corwin.

Knight, J. (2015). *Better Conversations: Coaching Ourselves and each other to be more credible, caring, and connected.* Corwin, A Sage Company.

Knight, J. (2017). *Impact Cycle.* Corwin Sage.

PLC at work®: Become a thriving Professional Learning Community. Solution Tree. (n.d.). Retrieved September 1, 2022, from https://www.solutiontree.com/our–solutions/plc–at–work

Positive parenting solutions & educational resources: Love and logic. Love and Logic Institute, Inc. (n.d.). Retrieved September 1, 2022, from https://www.loveandlogic.com/

Tate, M. L. (2010). *Reading and language arts: Worksheets don't grow dendrites* (2nd ed.). Corwin.

We've been researching and practicing instructional coaching for more than 20 years. Instructional Coaching Group. (n.d.). Retrieved September 1, 2022, from https://www.instructionalcoaching.com/coaching/

Whitaker, T. (2013). *What great principals do differently: Eighteen things that matter most (study guide).* Taylor and Francis.

About the Author

Ashley Hubner is an Instructional Coach and Curriculum Specialist who has served in many roles in education from elementary school teacher to Curriculum Lead. Her degrees include a Bachelor's in Elementary Education, a Master's in Curriculum and Instruction, and Principal Certification. She served 13 years in the public school system, then transitioned into an educational consultant role where she has worked with curriculum companies to build quality educational experiences for students and with school districts to build instructional capacity among staff.

Ashley's message about the importance of relationships resonates in everything she does; from volunteering at the local campus as a mom to working with corporate stakeholders. Ashley believes that our impact matters, no matter how big or small.

Contact Ashley for Coaching Support

If you need support in preparing coaches for their new roles or building a coaching framework to sustain coaching, reach out to ACCESS Coaching & Consulting founded by Ashley Hubner.

At any event she is a part of, Ashley brings her energy, passion and excitement to support instructional coaches in building instructional effectiveness within the classroom.

Services Include:
- Customized professional development
- Instructional Coaching
- Mentor Training
- PLC Team Coaching & Training

Website: https://coachingaccess.net/
Email: ashleyhubner@coachingaccess.net

132

More Books from Road to Awesome

- Road to Awesome: Empower, Lead, Change the Game by Darrin M. Peppard (via Codebreaker)

- Taking the Leap: A Field Guide for Aspiring School Leaders by Robert F. Breyer

- Transform: Techy Notes to Make Learning Sticky by Debbie Tannenbaum

- Becoming Principal: A Leadership Journey & The Story of School Community by Dr. Jeff Prickett

- Elevate Your Vibe: Action Planning with Purpose by Lisa Toebben

- #OwnYourEpic: Leadership Lessons in Owning Your Voice and Your Story by Dr. Jay Dostal

- The Design Thinking, Entrepreneurial, Visionary Planning Leader: A Practical guide for Thriving in Ambiguity by Dr. Michael Nagler

- Becoming the Change: Five Essential Elements to Being Your Best Self by Dan Wolfe

- inspired: moments that matter by Melissa Wright

Children's Books from Road to Awesome

- Road to Awesome A Journey for Kids by Jillian DuBois and Darrin M. Peppard

- Emersyn Blake and the Spotted Salamander by Kim Collazo

- Theodore Edward Makes a New Friend by Alyssa Schmidt

Made in the USA
Middletown, DE
09 January 2023

21253143R00084